100 EASY TALK THOUGHTS FOR LDS YOUTH

VOLUME TWO

100 EASY TALK THOUGHTS FOR LDS YOUTH
VOLUME TWO

Sandra & Joseph Harper

ISBN: 1-55517-445-0
v.2

Published by: **Bonneville Books**
Distributed by:

925 North Main, Springville, UT 84663 • 801/489-4084

CFI | Publishing and Distribution Since 1986

Cedar Fort, Incorporated

CFI Distribution • CFI Books • Council Press • Bonneville Books

Cover design by Corinne A. Bischoff
Printed in the United States of America

*Be ye therefore perfect even as your
father which is in heaven is perfect.*

Matthew 5:48

ACKNOWLEDGMENTS

We need to again thank Jackie Wynder, who waded through the raw beginnings of this work and gave encouragement as well as professional suggestions.

INTRODUCTION

Some might ask how we know if what we have taught in our books is of the Spirit and true. It has been stated by a great leader that he knew when he had taught by the Spirit because he had learned something he had not known previous to the experience. We have also learned much. To teach, by the Spirit, is awesome and enlightening.

In reading and using this book, it is essential to do so with the Spirit.

As with volume one, each section of this volume is opened with a question which we personally have heard asked or stated by someone.

We address these with the most precious insights to the gospel, making it a more adaptable and enjoyable part of our lives.

The purpose of all the symbolism, and the inter-dependence of each principle builds like a tree.

Like the tree there is a central trunk from which everything else extends. This trunk is Christ.

When we start with Christ in each of the gospel teachings we find how they all connect into one simple formula for life.

Part One

WHAT DID HE MEAN BY PERFECTION?

WHAT IS THE OIL?

HOW DOES KINDNESS IN SUFFERING BENEFIT US?

WHAT CAN MAKE PERFECTION POSSIBLE?

Almost everyday we hear someone say, "I'm not perfect." This is a common response to confrontations brought on by errors we make or a defensive barricade we set up to keep others from expecting too much from us.

If our perception of "perfection" is living without making errors, then of course we aren't perfect nor can we be. We are in a physically raw and imperfect state.

So what is the perfection asked for in Matthew 5:48? Is it possible to obtain it in this life? If so, what makes gaining this perfection possible?

Thought One
PERFECTION, RIGHTEOUSNESS, AND CHRIST

Christ is our Righteousness. Jeremiah 23:6 says:

> "In his days Judah shall be *saved*, and Israel shall dwell safely: and this is his name whereby he shall be called, *The Lord Our Righteousness*."

Christ, being *perfect*, is *righteous*. His *righteousness* is the power by which He takes upon Himself our sins and brings about our *righteousness* or *perfection*. 1 John 2:1 says:

> "My little children, these things write I unto you, that ye sin not, And if any man sin, we have an advocate with the Father, Jesus Christ *the righteous*."

When we have no sin, because we have repented of them, we are in a state of *righteousness or perfection* because the Savior has taken the sins from us. 2 Cor. 7:1:

> "Having therefore these promises, dearly beloved, *let us cleanse ourselves from all filthiness of the flesh and spirit, perfecting holiness in the fear of God*."

Wherever we see the word righteous in the scriptures, we can replace it with the words *perfection through Christ* because they are synonymous.

By understanding their synonymy we can simplify and understand exhortations of the scriptures to be *righteous or perfect. They are exhorting us to repent and allow Christ to take away our imperfections or unrighteousness, thus making us perfect or righteous.*

Refer to Moses 7:47; Romans 10:2-3; Isaiah 41:10; and Moroni 10:32-33.

OUR FIRST STEPS TO PERFECTION

Perfection defined as error, free living is virtually impossible. 1 John 1:8 says:

> "If we say that we have no sin, we deceive ourselves, and the truth is not in us."

But to become *righteous or perfect* through Christ, who atoned for our sins, is not. So in Matthew 5:48 we are commanded to:

> "Be ye therefore perfect, even as your Father which is in Heaven is perfect."

So what do we have to do in order for Christ to make us righteous? In Psalms 37:5-6 we are given three of the *first four* steps.

> *"Commit* thy way unto the Lord; *trust* also in him; and he shall bring it to pass. And he shall bring forth thy *righteousness* as the *light* and thy judgment as the noonday."

Before we can commit ourselves to Christ, we must, first, believe He exists. This is the first condition spoken of by King Benjamin in Mosiah 4:9 which says:

> "Believe in God; believe that he is, and that he created all things, both in heaven and in earth; believe that he has all wisdom, and all power, both in heaven and in earth..."

Step two is *commitment to Him in our hearts.* In this commitment we bind ourselves *to a certain course of action.* Mosiah 4:10-11 says in part:

> "And again, believe that ye must repent of your sins and forsake them, and humble yourselves before God..."

Also Acts 2:38 which says:

> "And he commandeth all men that they must repent, and be baptized in his name, having perfect faith in the Holy

One of Israel, or they cannot be saved in the Kingdom of God."

Step three, we add our *trust* or *hope in His work for us, committing our* eternal salvation into His care. Galatians 5:5 says:

> "For we through the Spirit wait for the hope of *righteousness* by faith."

Step four, He then *brings forth our righteousness by taking away our repented sins*. This He does because we are spiritually reborn to Him. Mosiah 27:25 in part says:

> "...(all people) must be...born of God, changed from their carnal and fallen state, to a state of *righteousness*, being redeemed of God becoming his sons and daughters;"

———◆———

Thought Three
A Changed Heart and Perfection

Anyone who has applied the *first four steps to perfection*, will have experienced a mighty change in their heart. Alma 5:13 says:

> "And behold, he preached the word unto your fathers, and a mighty *change* was also wrought in their *hearts*, and they *humbled* themselves and put their *trust* in the true and living God. And behold, they were *faithful* until the end; therefore they were *saved*."

Faith and hope in Jesus Christ brings about the *mighty change in our hearts,* after which, we experience the *fruit* of this *rebirth* when we are filled with *an impelling desire to be faithful to* Him. Ether 12:4 expounds upon what being *faithful* means. It says:

> "Wherefore, whoso *believeth in God* might with surety *hope* for a better world, yea, even a place at the right hand of God, *which hope* cometh of *faith*, maketh an anchor to the

souls of men, *which would make them sure and steadfast, always abounding in good works*, being led to *glorify God.*"

A changed or committed heart to Christ is evidenced by steadfastness, good works, and even more importantly, glorifying Him.

As we seek, first, *Christ's kingdom and His righteousness, which is the power to take away our sins,* we obtain perfection. Matthew 6:33 teaches us:

> "Seek ye *first* the kingdom of God, and His *righteousness;* and all these things shall be added unto you."

This is why we will have a compelling desire to not only perform all the good works, but also to glorify God.

> "For with God nothing shall be impossible."

> — Luke 1:37

Thought Four

BORN AGAIN THROUGH THE WORD OF GOD

Rebirth begins and ends with *The Word of God*. We must first *hear* about Jesus Christ through *His word, or the word of God*. We then must accept the Savior Himself who is also *The Word of God*. Revelation 19:13 records:

> "And he was clothed with a vesture dipped in blood: and his name is called *The Word of God*."

1 Peter 1:23 says;

> "Being born again, not of corruptible seed, but of incorruptible, by the word of God, which liveth and abideth forever."

The Word of God is *Christ and His word,* and *both liveth and abideth forever.*

Christ, being **The Word of God**, is *the way* to rebirth. Being b*orn again of Christ* is the *only* way we can be given the blessings of the atonement.

———————

THE PARABLE OF THE SOWER

The Word of God is expounded in the parable of the sower. The symbol of the seed is defined in Luke 8:11 which record:

"Now the parable is this: *the seed is the word of God.*"

Luke 8:4-8 gives us the metaphors of this parable:

"A sower went out to sow his seed and as he sowed, some fell by *the way side; and it was trodden down, and the fowls of the air devoured it.* And some fell *upon a rock; and as soon as it was sprung up, it withered away, because it lacked moisture.* And some fell *among thorns; and sprang up with it, and choked it.* And other fell *on good ground and sprang up, and bare fruit an hundred fold.* And when he had said these things, he cried, He that hath ears to hear, let him hear…"

The varied quality of ground in the parable represents people, at their different levels of preparedness, *to commit to Christ and His teaching*s. 8:12-15 continues:

"*Those by the way side* are they that hear; then cometh the devil and taketh away *the word out of their hearts, lest they should believe and be saved. They on the rock* are they, which when they hear, receive the word with *joy*; and these have *no roots*, which for a while believe, and in time of temptation fall away. *And they which fell among the thorns* are they, which, when they have heard, go forth, and are choked with cares and riches and pleasures of this life, *and bring no fruit to perfection. But that on the good ground* are they, which in an honest and good heart, having heard the word, keep it, *and bring forth fruit* with patience."

Whether it is *the word of God*, or *The Word which is God*, it is the same, if we are prepared to receive and commit to

Him and His words then *the seed* will grow from *rebirth* through *repentance* to the fruit of *perfection*.

Refer also to 1 Nephi 8:19; 15:23-24.

———◆———

Thought Six
NEPHI, THE SON OF HELAMAN

Nephi, the son of Helaman, was committed to the Lord even though he lived in some of the most dangerous and difficult times. Because of his *great faith in Christ* or *submissive heart* he was *steadfast*. In the book of Helaman 10:4-5 it records:

> "Blessed art thou, Nephi, for those things which thou hast done; for I have beheld how thou hast with unwearyingness declared the word, which I have given unto thee, unto this people. And thou hast not feared them, and hast not sought thine own life, but hast sought my will, and to keep my commandments. And now, because thou hast done this with such unwearyingness, behold, I will bless thee forever; and I will make thee mighty in word and in deed, *in faith and in works*; yea, even that all things shall be done unto thee according to thy word, for thou shalt not ask that which is contrary to my will."

Because of his *steadfastness* he was blessed. Not only was he given the power to do mighty works, he was also given the heavenly sealing power. These could only be given to him if he were *righteous*. Helaman 10:7 says:

> "Behold, I give unto you power, that whatsoever ye shall seal on earth shall be sealed in heaven; and whatsoever ye shall loose on earth shall be loosed in heaven; and thus shall ye have power among this people."

Nephi was just an ordinary person like each of us. The *quality* of commitment to the Savior entitled him to be made *righteous* or freed from his sins. We can also be made *righteous and blessed* through Christ.

Refer also to D&C 50:28-30

ANXIOUSLY ENGAGED

Perfection can only elude us if we lack *commitment or faith in our Savior which* is evidenced by a mighty change in our hearts. A changed heart brings forth the fruits of good works. D&C 58:27 teaches:

> "Verily I say, men should be anxiously engaged in a good cause, and do many things of their own free will, and bring to passed much *righteousness*."

Our Heavenly Father wants to see the evidence of our *changed heart or faith in Him. Repentance* is one of these evidences. If we are anxiously engaged in *repentance* we can bring to pass much *righteousness*, or, in other words, allow Christ's atoning power to make us perfect.

Thought Eight
COMMITMENT AND COVENANTS

A changed heart or faith in Christ is also evidenced by making *covenants*. Making covenants is part of being *steadfast in good works*. The fourth Article of Faith states:

> "We believe that the first principles and ordinances of the Gospel are: first, Faith in the Lord Jesus Christ; second, Repentance; third, Baptism by immersion for the remission of sins; fourth, Laying on of hands for the gift of the Holy Ghost."

The ordinance of baptism is *taken with covenants*. Mosiah 5:7 says:

> "And now, because of the *covenant* which ye have made ye shall be called the children of Christ, his sons, and his daughters; for behold, this day *he hath spiritually begotten*

you; for ye say that your *hearts are changed* through *faith* on his name; therefore, *ye are born of Him* and have become his sons and his daughters."

Thought Nine
IS KEEPING THE DO'S AND DON'TS ENOUGH?

Some think that if they are busy keeping all the do's and don'ts of the gospel that they are *righteous*. The Pharisees thought the same thing. In Luke 18:10-14 it says in part:

> "Two men went up into the temple to pray; the one a Pharisee, and the other a publican. The Pharisee stood and prayed thus with himself, God, I thank thee, that I am not as other men are, extortioners, unjust, adulterers, or even as this publican. I fast twice in the week, I give tithes of all that I possess."

But the Pharisee wasn't the one justified by the Savior.

> "And the publican, standing afar off, would not lift up so much as his eyes unto heaven, but smote upon his breast, saying God be merciful to me a sinner, I tell you, this man went down to his house *justified* rather than the other:"

A commitment to only the *do's and don'ts* of the gospel can't *justify*, therefore, they aren't enough. But our hearts can believe unto righteousness₁. Romans 10:10 in part says:

> "For with the heart man believeth unto righteousness…"

In other words, changed hearts which are committed to Christ and not just the do's and don'ts of His gospel are what justify us. James 4:8 teaches:

> "Draw nigh to God, and he will draw nigh to you. *Cleanse your hands*, ye sinners; and *purify your hearts*, ye double minded."

9

A committed heart *draws nigh to God*, and is not double-minded but is singly focused on Him. This is evidenced by *repentance*. Repentance is a spiritual act which *purifies* our hearts, and baptism is the physical act which *cleanses our hands*. D&C 121:33 says in part:

> "How long can rolling waters remain impure?..."

Rolling waters cannot remain impure. Neither can a *repentant and covenanted* heart. If we continue to move forward through continual repentance and good works, we too will become and stay purified as the *rolling* waters.

1. 100 Easy Talk, Vol. 2, thought One, pp.2.

Thought Ten
ALL THINGS IN WISDOM AND ORDER

Because the gospel is so all encompassing and asks so many things of us, it may appear to be more difficult than it needs to be.

The Lord does not expect more of us than we are able to accomplish. After all, who knows us and our potential better than He? Mosiah 4:27 says:

> "And see that all these things are done in wisdom and order; for it is not requisite that a man should run faster than he has strength. And again, it is expedient that he should be diligent, that thereby he might win the prize; therefore, all things must be done in order."

It is expedient that we be diligent, meaning constant in effort to accomplish something, but at a pace we can keep to win the prize.

We are also taught there is a time and season for all things. Ecclesiastes 3:1 says:

> "To every thing there is a season, and a time to every purpose under the heaven:..."

Also D&C 88:42 says:

> "And again, verily I say unto you, he hath given a law unto all things, by which they move in their times and their seasons…"

If we are:

- Obeying the commandments according to their proper time and season; receiving a change of heart, first, through submission to the Savior, who is righteousness;

- And are not running faster than we have strength;

we will be on the path of perfection and not be overwhelmed.

Thought Eleven
LEARNING FROM A BUTTERFLY

A butterfly, when it learns to catch the wind, doesn't have to work hard at all to go upward and onward.

The same is true of us and the gospel. The wind in our case is the *powers we gain* by having a *mighty change in our hearts*.

These powers are *faith and hope* in Christ which brings us to having the pure love of Christ, or *charity*. Galatians 5:4-5 & 14 say:

> "…For we through the Spirit wait for the *hope* of *righteousness by faith…for all the law is fulfilled in one word*, even in this; Thou shalt *love* thy neighbour as thyself."

When these three powers are left out, or we have not first experienced the mighty change in our hearts, the laws become *arduous* and without meaning. Galatians 5:4 says:

> "Christ is become of no effect unto you, *whosoever of you are justified by the law; ye are fallen from grace.*"

The performing of rituals without *faith and hope* in Christ and His saving power, weighs us down.

Gaining *faith, hope, and charity first,* precludes mean-ingless worship[1] and allows the Savior to lift us as the wind. 1 Corinthians 13:7 says:

> "...believeth all things, hopeth all things..."

It's like the butterfly catching the wind.

1. 1 Corinthians 13:2-3 or Thought Twenty-four

Section Two

WHAT IS FAITH, HOPE, AND CHARITY?

We have heard faith and hope used as though they were interchangeable. Are they the same? Has familiarity lessened our understanding?

We have also heard people describe "emotional" experiences as faith-promoting. What is the relationship between a surge of emotion such as joy, gratitude, or pride evoked by these experiences, and real faith producing power within our beings? What brings us to have true charity?

Thought Twelve
WHAT ARE FAITH, HOPE, AND CHARITY?

Other connotations are affixed to the words *faith, hope, and charity* so we will define them in the context of *gospel principles.*

We begin with *faith* which is the *belief* in Christ, His teachings, His power, and His love. When we say we believe all things, we are saying that we have *faith* in all things pertaining to Christ. Hebrews 11:6 says:

> "But without faith it is impossible to please him: for he that cometh to God must *believe that he is*, and that he is a rewarder of them that diligently seek him."

We then come to *hope* which is a *trust* in Christ and His atonement. The Webster's Dictionary defines hope as:

> "Desire with expectation of obtaining what is desired; trust."

When we say we *hope* all things, we are saying that we *trust* all things to Christ for our *eternal* salvation. Because of this trust, we are willing to make a *commitment* to Jesus Christ by *covenant*. Therefore we have *hope in covenants.*

Faith and hope allows the Spirit to *change our hearts. Changed hearts are filled with charity, the pure love of Christ,* which is emulated through being *honest, true, chaste, benevolent, virtuous, doing good to all men, and enduring all things.* Our *covenants* are kept through these things. The thirteenth Article of Faith says:

> "We believe in being honest true chaste, benevolent, virtuous, and in doing good to all men; indeed, we may say that we follow the admonition of Paul—We *believe* all things, we *hope* all things, we have *endured* many things, and *hope* to be able to *endure* all things. If there is anything *virtuous, lovely,* or of *good report or praiseworthy,* we seek after these things."

Our decree of *belief* encompasses all three *principles of faith, hope, and charity*, which are all essential components of a *changed heart* through Christ.

If we diligently seek to obtain these *principles of the gospel* we will be made new creatures in Christ or reborn. 2 Corinthians 5:17 says:

> "Therefore if any man be in Christ, he is a new creature: old things are passed away; behold, all things are become new."

Thought Thirteen
WHY IS FAITH FIRST?

In order to apply *faith, hope, and charity* to our lives, their interdependent workings and their correct order of acquisition needs to be understood.

Faith must come first. It is the foundation upon which hope is built. If we have not acquired *faith* or a belief that Christ exists first, then we can't have hope or put trust in Him or any of His works. Ether 12:18 says:

> "And neither at any time hath any wrought miracles until after their faith; wherefore they *first believed in the Son of God.*"

Miracles are part of His work. One of the greatest miracles is being reborn. Hebrew 11:1 says:

> "Now faith is the *substance* of things hoped for, the *evidence* of things not seen."

What is a substance (*assurance) or evidence which cannot be seen? Our forgiven sins and rebirth through Christ are substance and evidence that are not seen. Hebrews 11:3 gives us another. It says:

> "Through faith we understand that the worlds were framed by *The Word of God*[1] so that things which are seen were not made of things which do appear."

The worlds were framed by the unseen. So it is with faith. It is the *unseen foundation* or substance for hope.

Hope, which we confirm through *committing ourselves by covenants*, is the evidence of belief or unseen *foundation of faith* in Christ.

*The JST replaces substance with assurance.
¹Revelation 19:13

Thought Fourteen
WHY IS KNOWLEDGE NECESSARY?

The foundation of *faith, hope, and charity* is *knowledge*. The Bible Dictionary page 670 states:

> "All true faith must be based upon correct knowledge or it cannot produce the desired results."

Faith, hope, and charity, *without the knowledge of Christ*, do not exist. How could we have faith and hope in Him? If we knew not of Christ, how could we *obtain rebirth or charity which is His pure love*? Romans 10:17 says we gain faith from the word of God.₁

> "So then faith cometh by hearing, and hearing by the word of God₁."

Romans 15:4 speaks of scripture knowledge that gives us *hope*. It says:

> "For whatsoever things were written aforetime were written for our learning, that we through patience and comfort of the scriptures might have *hope*."

Hebrews 3:10 speaking of *knowledge and charity* says:

> "Wherefore I was grieved with that generation, and said, they do alway *err in their heart;* and they have not known my ways."

"They do alway err in their heart;" means they do not have charity, because they have not known or had knowledge of God's ways.

Without knowledge of God's ways there could be no faith or hope in them. Without faith and hope, there is no charity.

1   Revelation 19:13

Thought Fifteen

FAITH AND PRIESTHOOD

God is Jesus Christ. 2 Nephi 11:7 says:

> *"...BUT THERE IS A GOD, AND HE IS CHRIST, he cometh in the fulness of his own time."*

Priesthood is the power of God. *Faith* is the power upon which the *priesthood* is founded. 1 Peter 1:5 & 9 say:

> "Who are kept by the *power of God through faith* unto salvation ready to be revealed in the last time…Receiving the *end of your faith*, even *the salvation of your souls."*

There is no power for salvation without the priesthood. There is no access to the priesthood without *faith* or the *belief in Christ*.

So *faith* in Christ or the belief in His power to save us from our sins is the foundation of the Priesthood or the end of our *faith* unto salvation. Ephesians 1:19-20 also says:

> "And what is the exceeding greatness of his power to us-ward *who believe*, according to the working of his mighty power."

Binding covenants are made through priesthood ordinances. Without these *priesthood ordinances* we cannot be cleansed or *made godly* by the atonement. D&C 84:21 says:

> "And without the ordinances thereof, and the authority of the priesthood, the power of godliness is not manifest unto men in the flesh;"

Thought Sixteen

HOPE AND PATIENCE

Hope, through our *faith in and covenants with Christ*, gives us rest from the eternal burdens of our repented sins and imperfections. Acts 2:26-27 says:

> "Therefore did my heart rejoice, and my tongue was glad; moreover also my flesh shall *rest* in *hope*: Because thou wilt not leave my soul in hell, neither wilt thou suffer thine Holy One to see corruption."

In gaining *trust or hope in our covenants* with our Savior, we acquired the very important virtue of patience. Psalms 37:3 & 5-7 in part say:

> "Trust in the Lord, and do good…Commit thy way unto the Lord…Rest in the Lord, and wait patiently for him…"

We are not always blessed immediately, so it requires waiting. Waiting requires patience. 2 Peter 1:5-7 records:

> "And beside this, giving all diligence, add to your *faith* virtue; and to virtue *knowledge*; And to knowledge temperance; and to temperance *patience*; and to patience godliness; And to godliness brotherly kindness; and to brotherly kindness *charity*."

When we increase in our *faith and commitment* through *knowledge*, we develop *patience*. In *patience* we make greater *commitments* through *covenants*. Through these *covenants* we gain *hope*, and in *hope* we add other strengths.

When we *add to our faith*, we become fruitful in our knowledge of our Lord Jesus Christ. 2 Peter 1:8 says:

> "For if these things be in you, and abound, they make you that ye shall neither be barren nor unfruitful in the knowledge of our Lord Jesus Christ."

This emphasizes that *faith without works is dead,*[1] and works from these virtues demonstrates our knowledge *will not vanish away*[2] but will become fruitful.

1. James 2:26
2. 1 Corinthians 13:8

Thought Seventeen
WAITING AND PATIENCE

Galatians 5:5 says:

> "For we through the Spirit *wait* for the hope of *righteousness* by faith."

The hope of righteousness, confirmed through covenants, is in the atonement of Christ.

In *patiently waiting* for the Savior and *making covenants* with Him to bring about our *perfection*, we exercise *faith* which cultivates and enlarges *hope*. D&C 98:2-3 says:

> "Waiting patiently on the Lord, for your prayers have entered into the ears of the Lord of Sabaoth, and are recorded with this *seal and testament*—the Lord hath sworn and decreed that they shall be granted. Therefore, he giveth this PROMISE unto you, with an immutable *covenant* that they shall be fulfilled;..."

We are given an immutable *covenant*, in which we increase in *hope*, that if we *wait* with *patience* on the Lord, our blessings will be granted and *covenants* fulfilled. But there is more. Isaiah 40:31 says:

> "But they that wait upon the Lord shall renew their strength; they shall mount up with wings as eagles; they shall run, and not be weary; and they shall walk, and not faint."

In *patiently waiting* upon the Lord, we also receive *strength to endure.*

WHAT IS CHARITY

Charity is founded upon *faith* and *hope* in Christ. It grows from *the knowledge of, belief in, and hope for the work of Christ* in our behalf.

If we have *charity* we have been *reborn in Christ* and have received a *new heart* which is *filled with the pure love of Christ*. Moroni 7:47 says:

> "But charity is the pure love of Christ, and it endureth forever and whoso is found possessed of it at the last day, it shall be well with him."

Because *the Savior loved us first*, we have faith in Him and hope for our own eternal salvation and perfection through Him. We are therefore commanded to increase in love towards others. 1 John 4:19 & 21 say:

> "We love him, because he first loved us…And this commandment have we from him, That he who loveth God love his brother also."

Paul teaches us how we are to *love our brother* in 1 Corinthians 13:4-7 & 8 in part where he is defining charity; the pure love of Christ. He says:

> "Charity suffereth long, and is kind; charity envieth not; charity vaunteth not itself, is not puffed up. Doth not behave itself unseemly, seeketh not her own, is not easily provoked, thinketh no evil; Rejoiceth not in iniquity, but rejoiceth in the truth; Beareth all things, believeth all things, hopeth all things, endureth all things. Charity never faileth…"

Though dependent upon having *faith* and *hope* first, *charity* is the ultimate acquisition in being reborn. This brings us to obtaining a Christ-like quality of character or *perfection*. 1 Corinthians 13:13 says:

> "And now abideth faith, hope, charity, these three; but the greatest of these is charity."

When we have been reborn, or brought to have *charity*, we no longer have any desire to do evil. Mosiah 5:2 records:

> "And they all cried with one voice, saying: Yea, we *believe* all the words which thou hast spoken unto us; and also, we know of their surety and truth, because of *the Spirit of the Lord* Omnipotent, which *has wrought a mighty change* in us, or *in our hearts, that we have no more disposition to do evil*, but to do good continually."

Thought Nineteen
FAITH, HOPE, AND CHARITY VS. EMOTIONS

Some feel a swell of emotions during a spiritual experience and think they have grown in their faith, but the Bible Dictionary, page 670, states:

> "All true faith must be based upon correct knowledge or it cannot produce the desired results. Faith in Jesus Christ is the first principle of the gospel and is more than belief, since true faith always moves its possessor to some kind of physical and mental action;...A lack of faith leads one to despair, which comes because of iniquity."

True faith is evidenced by *action*. A lack of it brings despair. Ether 12:4 also expounds upon what happens to us when we experience *true faith and hope*. It says:

> "Wherefore, whoso believeth in God might with surety *hope* for a better world, yea, even a place at the right hand of God, which *hope cometh of faith*, maketh an anchor to the souls of men, which would make them *sure* and *steadfast*, always *abounding in good works*, being *led to glorify God*."

Faith, hope and charity are *evidenced* by steadfastness, good works, and even more importantly, glorifying God. Emotions, which come and go with experience-induced surges, are not.

21

When we try to replace *faith and hope* with emotions, we find that we are on a roller-coaster ride affected by changing circumstances. We are strong one day and weak the next, having *no steadfastness* in good works. We take pride in our ups and are devastated by our downs.

Though emotions are a very important part of who we are, they are not gospel principles which have any *power* for salvation through Christ. Alma 5:13 says:

> "And behold, he preached the word unto your fathers, and a mighty *change* was also wrought in their *hearts*, and they *humbled* themselves and put their *trust* in the true and living God. And behold, they were *faithful* until the end; therefore they were *saved*."

It is important to examine our behavior and judge whether we are just filling up with emotion or are actually being *changed in our hearts and strengthened by principles*.

———◆———

Thought Twenty
THE GOOD AND BAD OF EMOTIONS

Emotions can be good. Sorrow, for instance, can *prepare* us to seek out the Lord and repent. 2 Corinthians 7:10 in part says:

> "For godly sorrow worketh repentance to salvation…"

Sorrow which worketh *repentance* is an emotion derived from a *changed heart or rebirth*. It can guard us from losing our changed heart.

Emotions can also be *the joy we derive* after we exercise our *faith, hope and charity*. Acts 2:26-27 says:

> "Therefore did my heart *rejoice*, and my tongue was *glad*; moreover also my flesh shall *rest* in *hope*: Because thou wilt not leave my soul in hell, neither wilt thou suffer thine Holy One to see corruption."

Emotions and principles should work together to bring us to Christ. But they must be correctly identified as either *principles of power* according to steadfastness in good works and humility or *emotions,* which are only stepping stones to gaining and keeping *faith, hope and charity.*

Thought Twenty-one
TESTIMONIES OF SAND

If we substitute emotions for *faith, hope, and charity,* building our testimonies of Christ on emotional experiences alone, we are building them on sand.

But if we build our testimonies upon *principles of power,* we are building them on the *strong foundation of rock or Christ.* 3 Nephi 14:24-27 teaches:

> "...whoso heareth...and doeth them, I will liken him unto a wise man, who built his house upon a rock—And the rain...floods...and the winds...beat upon that house; and it fell not, for it was founded upon a rock. And every one that heareth...and doeth them not shall be likened unto a foolish man, who built his house upon the sand—And the rains...floods, and the winds...beat upon that house; and it fell, and great was the fall of it."

When our spiritual experiences have *humility, integrity in covenants, and charity* towards others, which does not slacken in difficult times, then we have increased in *faith, hope,* and *charity.* But if not, we have just experienced emotions.

Thought Twenty-two
SYMBOLS OF FAITH, HOPE, AND CHARITY

The Lord has always used symbols to help us understand His gospel. I have found three symbols that can represent *faith, hope, and charity* which bring their purposes into clear focus in the most simple and concise forms.

First, *faith. Faith is symbolized by a hot air balloon.* The balloon, lifted by the cleansing flames of *fire₁*, symbolizes our spirits being filled and lifted by *active faith in Jesus Christ.* 3 Nephi 13-15 records:

> "And it came to pass when they were all baptized and had come up out of the water, the Holy Ghost did fall upon them, and they were *filled* with the Holy Ghost *and with fire.*"

Second, *hope. Hope is symbolized by a rainbow.* Noah was given a *rainbow* as a sign of a *covenant* or promise between the earth and God. Genesis 9:13 records:

> "I do set my bow in the cloud, and it shall be for a token of a *covenant* between me and the earth."

We also have been given covenants, and in them we have hope. The *rainbow,* or *covenant of hope,* is essential to the work of Christ in our behalf and goes hand in hand with the *elevating balloon of faith.*

Third, *charity. Charity is symbolized by a heart,* meaning *charity* or the pure love of Christ. *Charity* is the ultimate element of *our changed hearts* which gives validity to our faith and hope. If we truly have acquired charity, then we will be able to answer the following questions in the affirmative. Alma 5:14 asks:

> "And now behold, I ask of you my brethren of the church, have ye spiritually been born of God? Have ye received his image in your countenances? Have ye experienced this mighty change in your hearts?"

The *heart* surrounding the *rainbow and balloon* represents the *validity of our belief and covenants with Jesus Christ through charity.*

If we have *charity* we will carry others up with us in our *faith-elevated* baskets, fulfilling our *hope-bearing* covenants in steadfast and good works. The heart is not only essential to the gospel of Jesus Christ, but is a powerful message for us.

The *balloon, rainbow, and heart* are the message of the gospel in three simple symbols. 1 Corinthians 13:13 says:

> "And now abideth faith, hope, charity, these three; but the greatest of these is charity."

1. D&C 19:31.

❧

WHAT IS FAITH WITHOUT WORKS?

———◆———

The need to increase in our faith is stressed so much today that many are looking for faith-promoting experiences. However, once they get what they think is an increase of faith, is what they do with it important?.

A young man in France received a strong witness of the truth of the gospel while being taught by the missionaries, but never consented to be baptized.

When asked why he wasn't baptized, he responded that he was waiting for another strong, spiritual witness of the truthfulness of the Church. Was his faith-promoting experience of any value without works?

Thought Twenty-three
FAITH WITHOUT WORKS

Faith, alone, which is a *belief in Christ*, will not work for our salvation. James 2:18-22 says:

> "Yea, a man may say, Thou hast faith, and I have works: shew me thy faith without thy works, and I will shew thee my faith by my works. Thou believest that there is one God; thou doest well: *the devils also believe*, and tremble. But wilt thou know, O vain man, that *faith without works is dead*? Was not Abraham our father *justified* by works, when he had offered Isaac his son upon the altar? Seest thou how faith wrought with his works, and *by works was faith made perfect?*"

Works by faith are necessary for both works and faith to be made perfect.

Works by faith unifies our *hearts and actions* in purpose and deeds so that *we can* be perfected or *complete*, which is the Hebrew meaning of perfect. This is the ultimate objective of our lives. James 2:26 says:

> "For as the body without the spirit is dead, so faith without works is dead also."

———

Thought Twenty-four
CAN OUR WORKS EARN SALVATION

We often hear we must *earn* our salvation through works, but what kind of works can we do which would produce so great a deed? Mosiah 2:21 says:

> "...I say, if ye should serve him with all your whole souls yet ye would be unprofitable servants."

If, no matter what we do, we are still unprofitable servants, then we cannot earn our own salvation. *We must trust in Christ for this.* But works derived from our *new heart in Christ* are necessary to prove our faith valid. James 2:21-22 again reminds us:

> "Was not Abraham our father justified by works, when he had offered Isaac his son upon the altar? Seest thou how *faith wrought with his works,* and by works was faith made perfect?"

Our works by faith are made perfect or *committed to Christ,* becoming works from the *pure love of Christ, or charity.* 1 Corinthians 13:3 says:

> "And though I bestow all my goods to feed the poor, and though I give my body to be burned, and have not charity, it profiteth me nothing."

So *only a faith in Christ which produces works,* induced by charity, profits us.

Thought Twenty-five
IS BELIEF ENOUGH?

We also hear that if we only believe or have faith in Christ our salvation will be sure. But James 2:14-17 says:

> "What doth it profit, my brethren, though a man say he hath faith, and have not works? can faith save him? Even so faith, if it hath not works, is dead, being alone."

Now *faith, being the foundation,* is necessary, but without the rest of the building, or the work, it is without worth. Also *works, being the building* without a foundation, or *works without faith,* is not only without value, but sin. Romans 14:23 says:

> "And he that doubteth is damned if he eat, because he eateth not of faith: for whatsoever is not of faith is sin."

Again James 2:22 says:

> "...and by works was faith made perfect?"

Thought Twenty-six
THE LORD WILL BE THE JUDGE

We may think because we are busy doing this and that, all will count for our eternal progress. But the Lord will judge whether our works are of Him or not. Samuel 2:3 says:

> "Talk no more so exceeding proudly; let not arrogancy come out of your mouth: for the Lord is a God of knowledge, and by him actions are weighed."

Romans 3:27 teaches us further that because our works must be based upon true faith in order to be effectual, that we can never boast in our works. It says:

> "Where is boasting then? It is excluded. By what law? of works? Nay: but by the law of faith."

Our dependence on the Lord for everything eliminates grounds for boasting, and increases the *value of faith, which encompasses works of charity.*

Thought Twenty-seven
PRIESTHOOD IS A WORK OF FAITH

Works of faith can be performed without priesthood, but *works of the priesthood* cannot be performed without *faith, because priesthood is a work of faith.*

Faith is the power upon which the *priesthood* is founded. 1 Peter 1:5 & 9 say:

> "Who are kept by the *power of God through faith...*"

There is no access to the priesthood without faith or the belief in Christ, so faith is the foundation of the priesthood.

Understanding that the *priesthood* is inseparably connected to *faith* brings us to a greater understanding of what the powers of faith and priesthood are and how they work together. An experience of the Savior's recorded, in Mark 5:27-30, 34 illustrates this further:

> "When she had heard of Jesus, came in the press behind, and touched his garment. For she said, If I may touch but his clothes, I shall be whole. And straightway the fountain of her blood was dried up; and she felt in her body that she was healed of that plague. And Jesus, immediately knowing in himself that *virtue* had gone out of him, turned him about in the press, and said, Who touched my clothes? ...And he said unto her, Daughter, *thy faith hath made thee whole* ; go in peace, and be whole of thy plague."

The woman accessed the healing *priesthood power, or virtue* of Christ, through her *faith*. Without her *faith*, *His virtue* could not have healed.

———————

FAITH AND OTHER CHRISTIAN CHURCHES

It is important to understand about faith and other Christian churches. The *works of faith* by themselves can be had by everyone who believes in Christ, whether they hold the priesthood or are in the Church of Jesus Christ of Latter-day Saints or not.

Faith is power through the belief in Jesus Christ. This is why Jesus told John not to forbid works of faith in His name just because they were not of His Church. Mark 9:37-40 say:

> "Whosoever shall receive one of such children in my name, receiveth me; and whosoever shall receive me, receiveth not me, but him that sent me. And John answered him, saying *Master, we saw one casting out devils in they name, and he followeth not us:* and *we forbad him, because he followeth not us, but Jesus said, forbid him not:* for there is no man which shall do a miracle in my name, that

can lightly speak evil of me. For he that is not against us *is on our part."*

Anyone who has *knowledge* of Jesus Christ and believes on Him can have the *power of faith in Him to do good works, even healings.* Moroni 7:33 says:

"And Christ hath said: If ye will have faith in me ye shall have power to do whatsoever thing is expedient in me."

With this understanding we should have regard and respect for all other Christian Churches and their works of faith as *they believe or have true and acting faith in Christ.*

However, though they may be able to have some of the blessings of faith in christ, we are given further revelation in D&C 76:71-72 that clearly tell us that their eternal progression is limited to the terrestial kingdom unless they accept the gospel in it's fullness. It says:

"And again, we saw the terrestrial world...whose glory differs from that of the church of the Firstborn who have received the fulness of the Father, even as that of the moon differs from the sun in the firmament. Behold, these are they who died without law."

In order to obtain the Celestial kingdom, they need the Melchizedek Priesthood, and the ordinances given under it's power. D&C 76:51-52&57 says:

"They are they who received the testimony of Jesus, and believed on his name...being buried in the water in his name...That by keeping the commandments they might be washed and cleansed from all their sins, and receive the Holy Spirit by the laying on of hands OF HIM WHO IS ORDAINED AND SEALED UNTO THIS POWER...And are priests of the Most high, after the order of Melchizedek, which was after the order of Enoch, which was after the order of the Only Begotten Son."

&

Section Four
WHAT IS THE OIL?

———————

In a Relief Society class, a sister made the comment that her extended family complained she was always busy. Then she added, "As members of the Church we are busy and that is the way it should be." However true this is, is being busy enough? Is there more to being a wise member of the Church than just being busy in Church work?

Thought Twenty-nine
THE TEN VIRGINS' LAMPS

We have all heard the parable of the ten virgins. It represents the potential outcome of the people of Christ's church. Matthew 25:1-2 say:

> "Then shall the kingdom of heaven be likened unto ten virgins, which took their lamps, and went forth to meet the bridegroom. And five of them were wise, and five of them were foolish."

The elements of this parable are the five wise virgins, the five foolish virgins, and their *lamps*.

The *lamps*, which are held by all the virgins, represents *membership in the Church*. In their membership, they are given access to all the covenants, ordinances and priesthood given to men on earth.

We all started out with equal blessings of Church membership, but what will make us wise members?

————◆————

Thought Thirty
TO BE ONE OF THE WISE VIRGINS

All ten virgins are *members of the Church*. Some are wise and some are foolish. The question is, what do we, as members, have to do to be one of the wise? Matthew 25:3-4 say:

> "They that were foolish took their lamps, and *took no oil* with them: But the wise *took oil* in their vessels with their lamps."

A wise virgin carried *a vessel of oil* as well as her *lamp of membership*.

————◆————

33

IS THE OIL FAITH?

Only the *wise* virgins brought more *oil* in a vessel. So what does the *oil* symbolize?

Some have speculated that the oil symbolizes our faith. But as Matthew 25:8-9 illustrates, that which gave the lamps *light* couldn't be shared. It says:

> "And the foolish said unto the wise, Give us of your oil; for our lamps are gone out. But the wise answered, saying, Not so; lest there be not enough for us and you: but go ye rather to them that sell, and buy for yourselves."

They are refused. Why? Can't faith be shared? Remember faith is the belief in Christ, His love and His power.

We often fast, pray and use the priesthood; and in these share our faith in behalf of others. Do we lose anything to ourselves when we do? No. In fact our faith only increases as we share it.

Even in Mark we are given an example of shared faith. A father, whose son was possessed of demons, brings him to the Savior to be healed but realizing he didn't have sufficient faith, asked the Lord to help his unbelief. Mark 9:24 records:

> "Jesus said unto him, If though canst believe, all things are possible to him that believeth. And straightway the father of the child cried out, and said with tears, Lord, I believe; help thou mine unbelief..."

In this example we are shown how faith can be shared with others who haven't sufficient faith of their own. So the oil isn't faith alone.

Thought Thirty-two
THE SYMBOLIC MEANING

The Lord never puts symbols into a parable unless they have significant hidden value. So what is the hidden symbolic value of the oil?

The oil, when used in lamps, can produce *light*. So the *oil* symbolizes our ability to produce *light*. Matthew 5:14 & 16 say:

> "Ye are the light of the world. A city that is set on an hill cannot be hid...Let your light so shine before men, that they may see your good works, and glorify your father which is in heaven."

By learning of our divine make-up, we also learn the significance of being able to radiate or produce light. D&C 93:29 teaches:

> "Man was also in the beginning with God. *Intelligence*, or the *light* of truth...."

Also D&C 93:36-37 says:

> "The glory of God is *intelligence*, or in other words, *light* and truth..."

The *oil* is our true intelligence or *light*. It can't be given away because it is the very essence of our being and the quality of person we are, and can become, through *correct application* of our knowledge, gifts, and talents[1]. D&C 130:18-19 say:

> "Whatever *principle of intelligence* we attain unto in this life, it will rise with us in the resurrection. And if a person gains more knowledge and *intelligence* in this life through his diligence and obedience than another, he will have so much the advantage in the world to come."

This *intelligence or light* is not only what gives us greater advantage in the world to come, but what others will see in us and cause them to glorify our Father in Heaven.

[1] 1 Corinthians 13:2,8. See also section six of *100 Easy Talk Thoughts for LDS Youth* Vol. I.

Thought Thirty-three
THE FOOLISH VIRGINS AND THE SLOTHFUL SERVANT

We are taught to let our light so shine that the Father may increase in glory[1]. The parables Jesus taught of both the foolish virgins and the slothful servant gave us the reason why. Compare their fates. First, the foolish virgins as recorded in Matthew 25:6 & 8:

> "While the bridegroom tarried, they all slumbered and slept. And at midnight there was a cry made, Behold, the bridegroom cometh; go ye out to meet him...And the foolish said unto the wise, Give us of your oil; for our lamps are gone out."

The slothful servant was like the foolish virgins in that he buried his talent and was also unprepared to demonstrate an increase when the Lord, who is symbolized as the *Lord and Bridegroom*, returned. Matthew 25:24-28 records:

> "Then he which had received the one talent came and said, Lord,...I was afraid, and went and hid thy talent in the earth: Lo, there thou hast that (which) is thine. His lord answered and said unto him, Thou wicked and slothful servant,...Take therefore the talent from him,..."

Having access to the gospel, which is represented here by *lamps and talents*, isn't enough. It is increasing what we have been given and receiving more which gives us an extra vessel of *oil* or an increase of *light*.

---

[1]Matthew 5:a6, also 100 Easy Talks, Vol. II, Thought 32.

Thought Thirty-four
THE OIL IS CHARITY OR TRUE INTELLIGENCE

Although true *intelligence* is based on *faith and hope*, it's more. It is the substance of who we are in terms of *charity* or being reborn. Moroni 10:21 says:

> "And except ye have charity ye can in nowise be saved in the kingdom of God."

In 1 Corinthians 13:4-8 Paul tells us what charity does:

> "Charity suffereth long, and is kind, charity envieth not; charity vaunteth not itself, is not puffed up, Doth not behave itself unseemly, seeketh not her own, is not easily provoked, thinketh no evil; rejoiceth not in iniquity, but rejoiceth in the truth; Beareth all things, believeth all things, hopeth all things, endureth all things. Charity never faitheth..."

Remember, *true intelligence* is charity and equals a change of heart or rebirth. 2 Corinthians 4:6 says:

> "For God, who commanded the *light*[1] to shine out of darkness, *hath shined in our hearts, to give light of the knowledge of the glory*[2] *of God in the face of Jesus Christ.*"

Alma 34:35 reinforces the message that *true intelligence* is *righteousness* or Christ in our hearts and this will be the *oil* we must have in order to dwell with the Savior.

> "...the Lord hath said he dwelleth not in unholy temples, but in the hearts of the righteous doth he dwell..."

When our hearts are *righteous*, repentant, and changed by the fullness of *charity*, then we gain greater portions of *light, true intelligence, or oil.*

[1] Matthew 5:14,16

[2] D&C 93:36-37

37

Thought Thirty-five
CHARITY ENDURETH

We know that the wise virgins had a goodly supply of *true intelligence or charity*, and thus it was well with them when Christ came. Moroni 7:47 says:

> "But charity is the pure love of Christ, and it *endureth* forever and whoso is found possessed of it at the last day, it shall be well with him."

Note here the kind of true intelligence or charity mentioned is an ability to endure. *Enduring* is what we have to do if we are to be the *wise prepared virgins* who were *patiently waiting* at the door when the bridegroom came to open it. Matthew 25:10 records:

> "And while they went to buy, the bridegroom came; and they that were *ready* went in with him to the marriage: and the door was shut."

The *foolish* could not *endure* because they were not *ready* with sufficient *oil* to wait.

Refer also to Isaiah 40:31

———◆———

Thought Thirty-six
WHAT WE COME TO BE

We who have the *oil* cannot share what we are. At that point we are what we have become, greater or lesser *intelligences* with greater or lesser spiritual *light to endure*. Alma 34:34 says:

> "Ye cannot say, when ye are brought to that awful crisis, that I will repent, that I will return to my God. Nay, ye cannot say this; for that same spirit which doth possess your bodies at the time that ye go out of this life, that same spirit will have power to possess your body in that eternal world."

See also D&C 88:27-32

We cannot share the amount of *true intelligence* or *charity* we have with another person. This only comes from each of our individual choices to obey the Lord's commandments during our lives. 1 Timothy 1:5 says:

> "Now the end of the commandment is charity out of a pure heart, and of a good conscience, and of faith unfeigned;"

If we have chosen to work at increasing our *light* to *endure* through love or charity, then we have our *vessel of oil* filled.

But if we did not so choose, then we will not have the *intelligence or light* to *endure* until the Savior comes.

See also section six of *100 Easy Thought Talks for LDS Youth,* Vol. I.

Thought Thirty-seven
A TIME TO PREPARE

Apparently those who made the effort to have *oil* did so before they all *slumbered*. Matthew 25:5 says:

> "While the bridegroom tarried, they all slumbered and slept."

The time of *slumbering* indicates *death* or the end of this life, which brought to an end the time to safely procure the *oil*.

We are only given a short time in which to gather our *oil and prepare* ourselves for the coming of *the Bridegroom*. Alma 34:31-34 say:

> "Yea, I would that ye would come forth and harden not your hearts any longer; for behold, now is the time and the day of salvation; and therefore, *if ye will repent and harden not your hearts, immediately shall the great plan of redemption be brought about unto you. For behold, this life is the time for men to prepare to meet God; yea, behold the day of this life is the day for men to perform their labors.* And now, as I said unto you before, as ye have had so many witnesses, therefore, I beseech of you that ye do not *procrastinate* the day of your *repentance* until the end; for after this day of life, which is given us to *prepare* for eternity, *behold, if we do not improve*

*our time while in this life, then cometh the night of darkness
wherein there can be no labor performed."*

Refer also to D&C 88:16-26.

Thought Thirty-eight
TO BE WISE OR FOOLISH

The *foolish virgins* will *procrastinate* until it is *too late* to
gather their *oil* and as Matthew 25:10-12 shows us, there will
be no time to go back and do what we should have already
done. It says:

> "And while they went to buy, the bridegroom came; and
> they that were ready went in with him to the marriage:
> and the door was shut...."

This life affords us the time and opportunities to increase
our true intelligence or *light*.

It is up to us to *wisely* procure sufficient *light to endure*
until the bridegroom cometh. Then we will be allowed to
enter into the wedding. Matthew 25:6-7 says:

> "And at midnight there was a cry made. Behold, the bride-
> groom cometh; go ye out to meet him. Then all those
> virgins (who were ready) arose, and trimmed their lamps."

Alma also tells of the admittance of *the righteous or wise* into
the wedding feast of Christ which represents *His kingdom.*
Alma 34:36 says:

> "...yea and he has also said that the *righteous* shall sit down
> in his kingdom, to go no more out; but their *garments should
> be made white through the blood of the Lamb."*

In order to be worthy to sit down in the kingdom; being
made *righteous* through Christ is essential.

WE CANNOT BE OVERCONFIDENT

The Savior teaches in the parable of the 10 virgins, that claiming the blessings of membership in His Church doesn't necessarily mean we will be ready with sufficient *enduring intelligence oil* to be accepted into His presence. Alma 34:35 says:

> "For behold, if ye have procrastinated the day of your *repentance* even until death, behold, ye have become subjected to the spirit of the devil, and he doth seal you his; therefore; *the spirit of the Lord hath withdrawn from you, and hath no place in you,* and the devil hath all power over you; and this is the final state of the wicked."

The wise will be more than just members of the Church, they will *repent and submit themselves to Christ continually to retain their pure heart and be prepared.*

Thought Forty
REPENTANCE TO KNOW THE LORD

Repentance plays a major part in receiving and retaining a changed heart. It conditions our hearts to submit to, and be known by, the Savior. And, in being known by the Savior, we increase in enduring light or charity. Matthew 25:11-12 records:

> "...Afterward came also the other virgins, saying Lord, Lord, open to us. But he answered and said, Verily I say unto you, I know you not."

Though we may appear to be busy doing the things that are right, if we are not *known by the Savior through daily submissive repentance* (for the Lord knows those whose sins he has taken upon Himself) keeping our hearts pure and full of charity we will not be able to *endure* and be admitted. Matthew 7:20-23 says:

"Wherefore by their fruits ye shall know them. Not every one that saith unto me, Lord, Lord, shall enter into the kingdom of heaven; *but he that doeth the will of my Father* which is in heaven. *many will say to me in that day: Lord, Lord, have we not prophesied in thy name? And in thy name have cast out devils? and in thy name done many wonderful works? And then will I profess unto them, I never knew you:* depart from me, ye that work iniquity."

Also 1 John 4:7-8 say:

"Beloved, let us love one another: for love is of God; and everyone that loveth is *born of God* and *knoweth God. He that loveth not knoweth not God; for God is love.*"

The wise will *come to know and be known by our Savior* through repentance and other actions that are *born from hearts full of charity* or *light*.

Thought Forty-one
REPENTANCE AND A HARDENED HEART

The *hardened* and *unsubmissive* heart is not repentant or full of charity, the pure love of Christ. Many times when we become too busy and consumed in what we can do, we become prideful and hardened in our hearts. Remember the Pharisee in Luke 18:10:

"The Pharisee stood and prayed thus with himself,—God I thank thee, that I am not as other men are, extortioners, unjust, adulterers, or even as this publican. I fast twice in the week, I give tithes of all that I possess."

To avoid becoming like the Pharisees in our actions, we, the wise members, will become *completely submissive to Christ, repentant and perfected through Him.* Matthew 5:48 says:

"Be ye therefore *perfect*, even as your Father which is in heaven is perfect."

Perfection through repentance and complete submission to Christ keeps our works free from pride and our hearts softened with love.

This kind of heart is the true *light* or intelligence oil the wise will work to gain in order to *endure* to the end, *perfecting the love of God.* 1 John 2:5 says:

> "But whoso keepeth his word, in him verily is the *love of God perfected:* hereby know we that we are in Him."

The parable of the ten virgins, combined with all these scriptures, teaches it isn't just membership in the church or faith that prepares us for entrance into the bridegroom's feast, but the condition of our hearts, knowing *we are in Christ.*

Or, in other words, to know that we have *been born again of charity* and, in so doing, possess sufficient *light* to *endure.*

❧

HOW DOES KINDNESS IN SUFFERING BENEFIT US?

———

A young sister had learned from her mother to always "do good for evil." So when her neighbors hurt her with untrue gossip, she had her children mow their lawn, and while she was watering her own lawn she would take an extra hour and water their dry spots. She found that as she served this neighbor her love for them increased and her pain disappeared. Forgiveness became easier. How can kindness in suffering benefit us?

Thought Forty-two
KINDNESS IN SUFFERING

1 Corinthians 13:4 says:

> "Charity suffereth long, and is kind;..."

1 Peter 2:20 says:

> "For what glory is it, if, when ye be buffeted for your faults, ye shall take it patiently? but if, when ye do well, and *suffer* for it *patiently*, this is acceptable with God."

We recover lost *light* when we suffer for our own folly, but suffering for doing well, as Christ did, reveals and increases inner spiritual strength or *true intelligence*. D&C 121:42 says:

> "By *kindness* and *pure knowledge*, which shall *greatly enlarge the soul* without *hypocrisy*, and without *guile*—"

Kindness is part of charity, and pure knowledge is truth. As *principles of intelligence*, they both reveal a change of heart or *enlarging of the soul*. The *enlarging of the soul is Christ in our hearts*. When we have Christ in our hearts, our characters become free of hypocrisy (falseness) and guile (craftiness).

Of all the *principles of intelligence* there are, these two combined, in being *kind in suffering* or having and *enduring love* in all circumstances, are most desirable.

Thought Forty-three
WORTH SUFFERING FOR

To have an *enduring love* in the worst situations, as well as the best, comes from the *enlarging of the soul* or charity.

Jesus set the example found in Mark 10:13. While He was teaching the people, some parents brought their children forward to have Him bless them.

"And they brought young children to him, that he should touch them…"

His disciples felt the interruption was inconsiderate and tried to turn the children away.

"…and his disciples rebuked those that brought them."

However, taking time to bless the children was a small *loss* which Jesus felt worth *suffering*, and so he countered His disciples rebuke. Mark 10:14 records:

"But when Jesus saw it, he was much displeased, and said unto them, *suffer* the little children to come unto me, and forbid them not: for such is the kingdom of God."

Jesus wasn't displeased with His disciples for trying to guard their Master, for they had seen Him worked many times to exhaustion. But He was displeased with their *lack of understanding*. So He set about to teach them, by example, what was most important and *worth suffering* for.

———◆———

Thought Forty-four
GREAT EXAMPLES

Jesus gave us the example of *long suffering and kindness*, not only in the small suffering of letting the children come to Him, but in the much greater sufferings of being beaten, spit upon, and crucified all with—

"Father, forgive them; for they know not what they do."

—Luke 23:34

—on his lips. He suffered all this to take upon Himself our sins. He had great *charity or enduring love* for us.

Though Christ was our greatest example, His prophets also gave us noteworthy example. 1 Nephi 3:28 & 29 say:

"And it came to pass that Laman was angry with me, and also with my father; and also was Lemuel, for he hearkened unto the words of Laman. Wherefore Laman and Lemuel did speak many hard words unto us, their younger brothers, and they did smite us even with a rod."

Nephi had suffered ridicule and had even been beaten by his brothers.

He could have felt sorry for himself or struck out in anger at his offenders or even at God, yet out of *enduring love*, he frankly forgave them. 1 Nephi 7:21 say:

"And it came to pass that I did frankly forgive them all that they had done, and I did exhort them that they would pray unto the Lord their God for forgiveness..."

———◆———

Thought Forty-five
THE PSALM OF NEPHI

In Nephi's Psalm, we are given an enlightening insight to how he deals with his *suffering*.

As he recognizes his *charity or enduring strength* is beginning to slacken because of afflictions, he calls upon his heart to rejoice, and no more give place for the enemy of his soul.

He rejuvenates this strength by turning from his troubles, which are draining his strength, to praying and praising God. 2 Nephi 4:29 & 30 say:

"...Do not slacken my strength because of mine afflictions. Rejoice, O my heart, and cry unto the Lord, and say: O Lord, I will praise thee forever; yea, my soul will rejoice in thee, my God, and the rock of my salvation."

By changing his focus, he is given strength of charity to endure.

As we search our scriptures, we find the power to *endure* difficulty, disappointment, or even severe suffering, comes by praising the Lord, and dwelling upon his goodness and mercies. In these our *charity* is preserved.

TRUSTING IN CHRIST

The *strength of charity* to *endure* pain and suffering was also acquired by Paul. Philippians 4:11-13 records his thoughts:

> "Not that I speak in respect of want: for I have learned, in whatsoever state I am, therewith to be content. I know both how to *be abased*, and I know how to abound: every where and in all things I am instructed both to be full and to *be hungry*, both to abound and to *suffer need*. I can do all things through Christ which strengtheneth me."

He proves his *enduring love or strength of charity* by being able to suffer or prosper, always being content in either. How does he do it? He trusts in Christ. He knows that Christ is his strength and will turn his suffering to good.

He doesn't deny there is suffering, he just transfers it into the power of Christ.

JOSEPH

Joseph, who was sold into Egypt by his own brothers, had great *enduring* love.

In his youth, he had been given a symbolic dream that his brothers would some day bow down to him. But they sold him into bondage instead.

He did not murmur or let this hardship take hold of his *heart*. Instead, he found his trust in the Lord. This gave him *strength in his charity* to resist temptations including the improper advances of Potiphar's wife. Genesis 39:9 illustrates this. It says:

"How then can I do this great wickedness, and sin against God?"

Though his *steadfastness* was not rewarded right away, and, in fact, caused his *suffering* to increase by being unjustly thrown into prison, he *endured* it all showing *charity* to those in prison with him.

One of the men in prison to whom he was kind eventually made him known to the king. Because he waited on the Lord, trusting in Him, his *kindness in suffering* or *charity* became the power whereby his prophetic dream was fulfilled.

His perspective and focus, from himself to God, and his *righteousness* made the difference. Genesis 41:16 illustrates Joseph's total *humility and trust* in the Lord for everything. It says:

> "And Pharaoh said unto Joseph, I have dreamed a dream, and there is non that can interpret it: and I have heard say of thee, that thou canst understand a dream to interpret it. And Joseph answered Pharaoh saying, *it is not in me: God shall give Pharaoh an answer of peace.*"

Thought Forty-eight
TURNING TO GOD

A *change of heart or charity* alters how we perceive our hardships and an altered perception changes our heart transforming it with *charity*.

This transformation is a turning from self-centeredness to looking out to God and His love for us. Thus we focus beyond ourselves and our circumstances, to He who is *love*. 1 John 7-8:

> "Beloved, let us love one another: for love is of God; and *everyone that loveth is born of God, and knoweth God...for God is love.*"

The change of heart or charity that occurs when we are *born again* is restored through repentance, loving one another, glorifying God, and rejoicing in His works for us.

The evidence of our charity is manifest in a show of *kindness* not only by uncommitted deeds of vengeance, blaming or recrimination against those who have caused our grief, but by forgiving and showing forth *love* in the face of suffering. It all comes from drawing nigh to God. James 4:8 says:

> "Draw nigh to God, and he will draw nigh to you. Cleanse your hands, ye sinner; and purify your hearts, ye double minded."

As we purify our hearts, obtaining charity, we can not only be strengthened in our afflictions, but we can stand before God with a clear conscience, and, in so doing, endure judgement. James 5:9 which says:

> "Grudge not one against another brethren, lest ye be condemned: behold, the judge standeth before the door."

Strength of *endurance and love* to put away our grievances come through the *change* of heart or *charity. In charity* we put off our own problems and are filled with *the strength of love* which is the strength of God.

———————

Thought Forty-nine
ROOTED IN CHRIST

If we are rooted in the *enduring love of Christ we will receive the change of heart*. It is through His love that we gain strength to *endure or suffer long* with no selfish expectations. Mark 4:3-8, the parable of the sower, powerfully demonstrates the importance of what we take root in. It says:

> "Hearken; Behold, there went out a sower to sow: And it came to pass, as he sowed, some *fell by the side*, and the fowls of the air came and devoured it up. And some *fell on stony ground* where it had not much earth; and immedi-

ately it sprang up, because it had no depth of earth: But when the sun was up, it was scorched; and because it had no root, it withered away. And some *fell among thorns*, and the thorns grew up, and choked it, and it yielded no fruit.. And others *fell on good ground* and did yield fruit that sprang up and increased ; and brought forth, some thirty, and some sixty, and some an hundred."

Notice how each time the seed was not in *good ground* it did not *endure* to fruition.

If we plant our hearts carelessly falling by the side into Satan's way, he will snatch us up, using us to promote himself. If we plant in stony or *selfish* soil, it will have nothing to feed on but itself and will be scorched when trials and hardship come. Likewise, if we plant in the thorny or *worldly soil*, it will choke us with its cares, deceits and riches, and we will yield no fruit. However, if we plant in the good ground, we will grow and give much fruit.

———————

Thought Fifty
THE GOOD GROUND

Christ is the *good ground*. Rooting our hearts in Him gives us much fruit. The fruit is the power to *enlarge our souls and strength to endure with love* in any and all hazards of life. Colossians 2:6 & 7 say:

"As ye have therefore received Christ Jesus the Lord, so walk ye in him: Rooted and built up in him and established in the *faith*, as ye have been taught, abounding therein with thanksgiving."

If we are in Christ, *our long suffering or enduring with love* will fill us with thanksgiving.

It will not just be a holding on as time passes. It will be a genuine strength-building experience.

———————

Thought Fifty-one
FALSE MARTYRS

If we suffer for *sympathy and praise of men,* as *false martyrs* do, we will not have the real, *enduring love,* but a *counterfeit.*

To claim this *principle of enduring love,* our suffering and endurance are authentic. Genuine *endurance* comes from a *new heart* that has certain *qualities* and *bears* fruit. It won't be just waiting for time to pass or an act for pity and self-aggrandizement.

There are two kinds of *fruits* reaped when a *principle of intelligence* is obtained. First; *the change of heart* or a *characteristic of charity* which is the *quality fruit,* and second, the *eternal reward fruit.* Hebrews 6:15 says:

> "And so, after he had patiently endured, he obtained the promise."

Patience, being a characteristic of charity is the quality fruit, and obtaining the promise is the *reward fruit.*

———

Thought Fifty-two
ENDURE CHASTENING

Another kind of *enduring* is found in Hebrews 12:5-7 & 10. It also has a *quality fruit* and a *reward fruit.* The scripture reads:

> "And ye have forgotten the exhortation which speaketh unto you as unto children, My son, despise not thou the chastening of the Lord, nor faint when thou art rebuked of him: For whom the Lord loveth he chasteneth, and scourgeth every son whom he receiveth. If ye *endure chastening,* God dealeth with you as with sons; for what son is he whom the father chasteneth not? For they verily for a few days chastened us after their own pleasure; but he for *our profit, that we might be partakers of his holiness.* Now no chastening for the present seemeth to be joyous, but grievous:

nevertheless afterward it yieldeth the *peaceable fruit of right-eousness* unto them which are exercised thereby."

There will be those that *chasten us after their own pleasure* which would require the *quality of patience* in our *endurance.*

But the Lord, who chastens *for our profit that we might be partakers of his holiness,* would require more.

To endure chastening from God is having the *quality fruit of humility* which turns us to Him through repentance. This yields the *peaceable reward fruit of righteousness, which is Christ's bringing about our perfection.*

———————◆———————

ENDURING FAITH

An *enduring faith* is found in D&C 101:35 which says:

> "And all they who suffer persecution for my name, and endure in *faith,* though they are called to lay down their lives for my sake yet shall they partake of all this glory."

This *endurance is of our faith in Christ* to the point of even *laying down our lives for His sake.*

The *quality fruit is the ability to endure all things.* The *reward fruit is partaking of this glory* that will be of the Father's kingdom.

———————◆———————

SUFFERING TEMPTATIONS

True suffering of temptations also is proved by two kinds of *fruits.* James 1:12 says:

> "Blessed is the man that endureth temptation: for when he is tried, he shall receive the crown of life, which the Lord hath promised to them that love him."

Being *tempted and tried* is the *quality fruit* because it challenges our *enduring love or inner strength*.

Through this trying we may know, with certainty, whether we have sought false martyrdom or truly *loved Christ and received His quality of enduring love*.

If we are found having *true enduring love or charity* in the heat of trial, then we *shall receive the crown of life*, the *reward fruit*.

Thought Fifty-five
UNTIL THE END

The next progressive step in gaining greater endurance is found in 3 Nephi 15:9 which says:

> "Behold, I am the law, and the light. Look unto me, and *endure to the end*, and ye shall live; for unto him that endureth to the end will I give eternal life."

Now if we have *endured with charity, having patience in chastening, faith in Christ, enduring temptation and trial*, and we continue to do so *until the end*, then we have the *quality fruit of steadfastness*, and we will receive the *reward fruit of eternal life*.

Thought Fifty-six
ENDURING WELL

Finally, the *ultimate endurance* goes beyond *enduring to the end, tests of patience, chastening and faith*. If we show forth even greater proof of our love for our Savior by loving our foes, we will have endured *well*. D&C 121:8 says:

> "And then, if thou endure it well, God shall exalt thee on high; thou shalt triumph over all thy foes."

If we have *endured steadfastly, magnifying* our strength and *kindness beyond what was asked of us*, then we have not only endured it, we have *endured it well*. It means *going the extra mile*. Matthew 5:39-48 teaches us:

> "But I say unto you...whosoever shall smite thee on thy right cheek, turn to him the other also. And if any man will sue thee at the law, and take away thy coat, let him have thy cloke also. And whosoever shall compel thee to go a mile, go with him twain.... Ye have heard that I hath been said, Thou shalt love thy neighbour, and hate thine enemy. But I say unto you, Love your enemies, bless them that curse you, do good to them that hate you and pray for them which despitefully use you, and persecute you; *that ye may be the children of your Father which is in Heaven:* for he maketh *His sun to rise on the evil and on the good*, and sendeth rain on the just and on the unjust. For if ye love them which love you, what reward have ye? do not even the publicans the same? And if ye salute your brethren only, what do ye more than others? do not even the publicans so?"

In doing more than is required, we have truly acquired the greatest level obtainable in these *principles of charity or kindness in suffering. We become children of our Father in Heaven.*

Then we would be the Celestial quality of people. The people whose kingdom is compared to the Sun[1]. The Sun which, without judgment shines on both the good and the evil.

[1] D&C 76:70

Thought Fifty-seven
To Suffer Great or Small

To suffer is to endure a loss or difficulty of any description, large or small.

To be kind is to accord service, friendship, support, understanding, and forgiveness with love.

To be long suffering and kind is to accord an *enduring love* in all that we do, or in other words have *charity*.

To be proven genuine in *enduring with love* earns for us an eternal character or perfection as its fruit.

In turning to our Lord and Savior for strength, praying to the Father through Christ, we can say as Paul says in Philippians 4:13:

> "I can do all things through Christ which strengtheneth me."

Remember Moses 1:39 says:

> "For behold, this is my work and my glory—to bring to pass the immortality and eternal life of man."

Truly it is by the strength of God that our perfection is accomplished and to Him is the glory and honor and power, forever.

Why Must We Depend on the Lord?

WHY IS THE WAY WE THINK IMPORTANT?

A sister often noticed that without any apparent reason people whom she had felt close to would suddenly avoid her, or give her the cold shoulder. After suffering tremendous, emotional pain from these unexplainable occurances, she fasted and prayed for several days. It was the conclusion of this fast that she had a dream.

In this dream she received the "Parable of The Three Sisters." (found in Thought 67) This parable explained that what was happening to her was not her fault, but the fault of gossips both in and out of leadership. Does what we say about others affect the way they are thought of and treated?

Thought Fifty-eight
AS YE THINK

In Corinthians 13:5 we are taught that:

> "...(Charity) thinketh no evil...."

Paul taught the Corinthians to *think no evil* and in Proverbs we find out why. Proverbs 23:7 teaches:

> "For as he thinketh in his heart, so is he;..."

This truth is reiterated in an old, Scottish saying which goes something like this:

> "Sew a thought, reap an act, sow an act, reap a habit, sow a habit, reap a character, sow a character, reap an eternal destiny."

We are on earth to increase in intelligence or charity, and our *thoughts* affect the eternal destiny we will reap. Therefore, its important to be selective about what *thoughts* we allow into our minds.

Thought Fifty-nine
LEAD US TO CHRIST

In Philippians 4:8, Paul teaches us what our *thoughts* should be centered on. It says:

> "Finally, brethren, whatsoever things are true, whatsoever things are honest, whatsoever things are just, whatsoever things are pure, whatsoever things are lovely, whatsoever things are of good report; if there be any virtue, and if there be any praise, *think* on these things."

As he admonishes us to think on things which are *true, honest, just, pure, lovely, of good report, of virtue or of praise, he is leading us to the feet of our Savior* who is all these things. The passage in D&C 6:36 simplifies what Paul taught. It reads:

> "Look unto me (Christ) in every thought; doubt not, fear not."

Thought Sixty
PEOPLE ARE THE REASON

People are the reason we are to look unto Christ and His gospel. All the gospel principles teach us to have *right thoughts or love* in our relationships with one another. Proverbs 12:5 in part teaches us:

> "The thoughts of the righteous are right;...."

When we have right *thoughts,* our relationships increase in love. We look for the best or *think* pleasant, uplifting *thoughts* about each other. In other words, we increase in *charity.* Proverbs 15:26 continues to teach us:

> "The thoughts of the wicked are an abomination to the Lord..."

When we have wicked *thoughts,* our relationships become selfish, critical and loveless, becoming an abomination to the Lord.

Thought Sixty-one
FIRST PRIORITY

It is important, through our *thoughts,* to keep all facets of the gospel in their correct priorities.

In Christ's day the *thinking* of the people caused them to make the laws more important than the people they served. Because their *thoughts* inverted the priorities, the laws became enslaving and destructive instead of beneficial.

The Savior taught the priority of *man and law* in this quote found in Mark 2:27. It says:

> "And he said unto them, The sabbath was made for man, and not man for the sabbath:"

In spite of the Savior's teachings that *man was more important than law*, the Jewish members of the church *thought* because of their obedience to the *law* of circumcision, they were superior to the Gentile members. By so thinking, they lacked *the more important qualities of love or charity* in their obedience.

Thought Sixty-two
WHAT'S THE TRUE PURPOSE?

The Lord justifies both Jew and Gentile if they experience the *true purpose* of the laws and ordinances which is a *change of heart*.

The Jews *thought* the laws and ordinances had priority over the *change of heart*. Romans 2:14-15 gives us an example of this:

> "For when the Gentiles, which have not the law (circumcision), do by nature the things contained in the law, these, having not the law are a law unto themselves: *Which shew the work of the law written in their hearts, their conscience also bearing witness*, and (the Jews) their *thoughts, the mean while, accusing or else excusing one another;*"

The laws and ordinances written in their hearts validated them. Otherwise they would profit them nothing. Galatians 5:2&6 say:

> "Behold, I Paul say unto you, that if ye be circumcised, Christ shall profit you nothing...For in Jesus Christ neither circumcision availeth anything, nor uncircumcision; but *faith* which worketh by *love*."

We, also, find that our ordinances are validated through faith and love. So *thinking* otherwise can cause us to lose the very thing we *think* we are gaining.

OUTWARD OR INWARD

The Savior stressed the importance of making ourselves more pure. Therefore we perform our *outward ordinances* such as baptism to wash our sins away. However, the real work is within our *thoughts* and hearts, to count. Luke 11:39 says:

> "And the Lord said unto him, Now do ye Pharisees make clean the outside of the cup and the platter; but your inward part is full of ravening and wickedness."

Many stress the ordinances in their application of religion, but take little or no *thought* for the condition of their hearts. But if our ordinances and obedience to laws are to benefit us eternally, then we will *change within* also. Psalms 24:3-4 records:

> "Who shall ascend into the hill of the Lord? or who shall stand in his holy place? He that hath clean hands, *and a pure heart*; who hath *not* lifted up his soul unto vanity, or sworn deceitfully."

The Pharisees' *thoughts* of superiority in their obedience to laws and ordinances caused their hearts to become *vain and impure,* therefore *renduring* their obedience ineffective. The right thinkers will guard against the same.

Refer also to Matthew 23: 25: 28.

Thought Sixty-four
CHARITY AND OUR THOUGHTS

As in all our doctrines, *charity*, the pure love of Christ, is the ultimate goal. Therefore, charity is especially important in our *thinking*.

When we lack *charity* in our *thinking* about others because of pride in our obedience to laws and ordinances, we lose the message of Christ's life and mission. 2 Corinthians 10:7 asks us to look at the way we judge others in our thoughts:

> "Do ye look on things after the outward appearance? If any man trust to himself that he is Christ's, let him of himself *think* this again, that, as he is Christ's, even so are we Christ's."

Think: Others, in or out of the church, who do not have the blessings of temple ordinances, may be just as dedicated to the Savior as we are. Rather than judging others by what they do or don't have in the way of laws and ordinances, we can focus on the two great things we have in common, which are:

First: *We are all children of our Heavenly Father,* and

Second: *He loved us all enough to send His Son Jesus Christ.*

These two truths will help our *thoughts* to be of loving one another, and living the higher law of *charity.*

Thought Sixty-five
HOW WE USE IT

We cannot *think* because we have been given much, that we can point a condescending finger toward any who do not have everything we have. Luke 12:48 says:

> "But he that knew not, and did commit things worthy of stripes, shall be beaten with few stripes. *For unto whomsoever much is given, of him shall be much required:* and to whom men have committed much of him they will ask the more."

Many great prophets and even the Savior Himself taught it is not *what* we have been given in the way of laws and ordinances that makes us more worthy, but *how* we use what we have to increase *charity* in our *judgment and actions towards* others. Romans 12:13 explains:

"For I say, through the grace given unto me, to every man that is among you, *not to think of himself more highly than he ought to think;* but to *think soberly,* according as God hath dealt to every man the measure of faith."

When we, as Paul, recognize that we have been given our faith through the grace and mercy of the Lord, then we won't think too highly of ourselves, but will be filled with love and compassion for those who have been given less.

Refer also to Matthew 21:28-32.

Thought Sixty-six
THOUGHTS OF LOVE

All the prophets and apostles have taught us to consider our *thinking* about ourselves and others with compassion and love, especially toward sinners. Galatians 6:1-3 says:

"Brethren, if a man be overtaken in a fault, ye which are spiritual, restore such an one in the spirit of meekness; considering thyself, lest thou also be tempted. Bear ye one another's burdens, and so fulfill the law of Christ. For if a man *think himself to be something, when he is nothing, he deceiveth himself.*"

D&C 38:24-25 reiterates the commandment to love our neighbor as ourselves. We *gain love for ourselves* by loving others. It says:

"And let every man esteem his brother as himself, and practice virtue and holiness before me. And again I say unto you, let every man esteem his brother as himself."

As we follow these commandments, we begin to *think* more respectfully of ourselves and others, and then our *thoughts* are revealed in loving actions.

Thought Sixty-seven
OUR ACTIONS REVEAL OUR THOUGHTS

The following parable gives us a picture of how our thoughts are revealed in our actions:

> *PARABLE OF THE THREE SISTERS...The first story: There were three sisters. Two were standing in the foyer of the church, conversing together, when they saw the third approaching. The one sister said to the other, "We really don't want to be around her, she has so many problems. Let's just say hello and excuse ourselves."*

> *When the third sister came up to them, she had a pleasant smile on her expectant countenance. She greeted them warmly with, "I've had a long week, how about you?"*

> *Instead of responding to this sister with love and support, they hurriedly gave excuses for leaving and left her standing there hurt and bewildered.*

> *The second story: There were three sisters. Two were standing in the foyer of the church conversing together when they saw the third approaching. The one sister said, to the other, "This sister is really a great lady, but she has had it really rough lately. Let's see if there is anything we can do to help her."*

> *When the third sister came up to them, she had a pleasant smile on her expectant countenance. She greeted them warmly with, "I've had a long week, how about you?"*

> *The two sisters responded lovingly, sharing her difficulties. In empathizing with her they found answers to some of her problems. This fellowshipping not only increased their love and respect for one another, but bonded them in true sisterhood.*

Though the outcome of both stories were totally different, the sister with problems was the same in both.

The difference was made in how the two sister *thought* or were made to *think* of the third. Making one *think* kind or unkind things of the other decided the *actions* towards her.

Thought Sixty-eight
POWER TO LIFT

The way we *think* about and treat others has a profound affect on their spiritual progress as well as our own.

Think: We are *all* beings of intelligence. Abraham 3:22 says:

> "Now the Lord had shown unto me, Abraham, the intelligences that were organized before the world was..."

As intelligences we are clothed with a corruptible or mortal shell of weaknesses, both of body and character. 2 Corinthians 4:7 says:

> "But we have this treasure in earthen vessels, that the excellency of the power may be of God and not of us."

Our physical bodies are the earthen vessels, and the excellency is the Light of Christ which is of God. In Ether 12:27 we are taught that our weaknesses in our bodies and characters are given to us by God. Ether 12:27 says:

> "And if men come unto me I will show unto them their weaknesses. I give unto men weaknesses that they may be humble; and my grace is sufficient for all men that humble themselves before me; for if they humble themselves before me, then I will make weak things strong unto them."

We cannot *think* these weaknesses are *who we are*. They are solely challenges, given to us by God, to make us humble, so He can help us make them into strengths.

They aren't to identify individuals by, nor to justify uncharitable behavior. They are things we *all* must overcome.

If we *think* about and treat others *uncharitably* because of their weaknesses, then we make it more difficult for them and ourselves to overcome the challenges.

A CHOICE

Our choice to pollute others *thoughts* with hurtful gossip or to lift others *thoughts* with pleasant words is already made by what we have filled our minds with.

Remember, to share uplifting *thoughts* empowers all with *loving thoughts*. But to share hurtful *thoughts* burdens all with *selfish and destructive thoughts*.

Choosing to fill our *thoughts* with lifting power is especially important for those in positions of leadership.

Since the church is one of lay leadership, most everyone has had or will have opportunity of being a leader. When we are in these positions, we have a much greater power to aid or injure the progress of others.

Therefore, while we are in leadership and forever after, it is important to take heed to keep and never share, *unnecessarily*, confidences with spouses or other leaders.

Always seeking to represent everyone within our *stewardship* and within our circle of influence in the best light to others facilitates their progress and ours.

In this way, we are not only *righteous* in our *thoughts*, we help others to be uplifting in their *thoughts* also.

How we *think* or are made to *think* about others affects us all, and ultimately all our ability to love ourselves and to live better. Proverbs 23:7 says:

"For as he thinketh in his heart, so is he..."

IRRETRIEVABLE DAMAGE

We can do irretrievable damage if we *think* to injure instead of lift. Just think of a pillow full of feathers being strewn about on a windy day. How possible would it be to retrieve all the feathers back again? What would happen?

Following is a brief example of what happened to a victim of untrue accusations.

> *THERE WAS A MAN who had someone bring serious accusations against him in a church court. In the investigation he was found to be totally innocent. In fact, he wasn't even in the country when the incident was supposed to have happened.*
>
> *Forty years later this man's name came up for an important calling. Though the accusations had all been proven to be false, those who had been in the investigation found themselves with unwanted thoughts and doubts about the man. They knew he was innocent, but the untrue accusations were still burdening their thoughts.*

When we are brought to *think uncharitably* of anyone's reputation, though it be unjust, permanent damage is done.

On the other hand, when the accusations prove to be true, we may *think* that we are justified in treating *the accused* coldly because we *think* him less than respectable. We forget that he is a child of God.

The Lord gave us the "Sermon on The Mount" to teach us to treat even our enemies with love and kindness. Matthew 5:44 teaches:

> "But I say unto you, Love your enemies, bless them that curse you, do good to them that hate you and pray for them which despitefully use you, and persecute you;"

He also set the example of *thinking charitably by defending, and fellowshipping,* with the publicans, sinner, and the poor. He even prayed for those who despitefully used Him and persecuted Him. Luke 23:34 records that prayer:

"Father forgive them; for they know not what they do."

He recognized their need for His succor. *Remember, charitable* uplifting of others lifts us also.

Thought Seventy-one
WHAT THINK YE OF CHRIST?

A major *thought*, provoking question to ponder, which has greater impact on our behavior than any other, is found in Matthew 22:42 which asks:

"…What think ye of Christ?…"

The way we *think* of Christ determines our *thoughts* which determines the way we live. Isaiah 55:7-9 says:

"Let the wicked forsake his way, and the unrighteous man his thoughts: and let him return unto the Lord, and he will have mercy upon him; and to our God, for he will abundantly pardon. *For my thoughts are not your thoughts,* neither are your ways my ways, saith the Lord. For as the heavens are higher than the earth, so are my ways higher than your ways, and my thoughts than your thoughts."

If we fall short, God will have mercy on us as we continually *repent* and strive to fill our thoughts with *charity*.

Because it is through our *thoughts* that we make our judgments, when we temporarily consider some unrighteous thing, our *thoughts* can process these out of our behavior, and we overcome the temptation.

These temporary unrighteous *thoughts* can be forgiven. Acts 8:22 says:

"Repent therefore of this thy wickedness, and pray God, if perhaps the thought of thine heart may be forgiven thee."

Thought Seventy-two
DAVID'S ADVICE TO SOLOMON

Solomon was taught by David in 1 Chronicles 28:9. It says:

> "And thou, Solomon my son, know thou the God of thy father, and serve him with a *perfect heart and a willing mind:* for the Lord searcheth *all hearts,* and understandeth all the imaginations of the *thoughts:* if thou seek him, *he will be found of thee;* but if thou forsake him, he will cast thee off for ever."

Our thoughts show whether or not we have Christ with us. Therefore, they are of primary importance where our eternal salvation is concerned. Mosiah 4:30 says:

> "But this much I can tell you, that if ye do not watch yourselves, and your *thoughts* and your words, and your deeds, and observe the commandments of God, and continue in the faith of what ye have heard concerning the coming of your Lord, even unto the end of your lives, ye must perish. And now, O man, *remember,* and perish not."

Thought Seventy-three
THOUGHTS TO REMEMBER

Our thoughts also come in the form of remembrances. We covenant in our sacramental prayer to always *remember Him,* meaning Christ. The above scripture admonished us to *"remember* and perish not."

So watching what we feed our minds, centering our thoughts on Christ, we create these *thoughts* to *"remember."*

It takes a conscientious effort to have *thoughts* that give us spiritual power and to *remember* them. D&C 121:45 says:

> "Let thy bowels also be full of *charity* toward all men, and to the the household of faith, and *let virture garnish thy thoughts unceasingly;* then shall thy confidence wax strong

71

in the presence of God; and the doctrine of the priesthood shall distill upon thy soul as the dews from heaven."

If we are *virtuous thinkers*, when we are in the presence of God, we will have confidence in our *thoughts* being pure and not found wanting in virtue.

We are also given an increased understanding of priesthood doctrine. The priesthood is the power of Christ. So we increase in the doctrines of Christ's power. These are doctrines which are power unto salvation, or perfection.

Thought Seventy-four
THINKING ON CHRIST

Everything that comes from our *righteous thoughts* brings us forward to an increase of Christ, who is *righteous*, in our lives.

Remember, Paul admonished us to *think* on uplifting things[1] which is the same as *thinking* on Christ.[2] Malachi 3:16 says:

> "Then they that feared the Lord, spake often one to another: and the Lord hearkened, and heard it, and a book of Remembrance was written before him for them that feared the Lord, and that *thought upon His name.*"

To *think* upon the Lord and direct our *thoughts* in virtuous paths, gives us a *remembrance* which increases our *glory, or intelligence.*

The Lord, also, is keeping a written *remembrance* wherein we will be judged.

[1] Phillipians 4:8. See also Thought Sixty in *100 Easy Thought Talks for LDS Youth,* vol. I.
[2] D&C 6:36

Thought Seventy-five
SUMMARY

Our *thoughts* precede our actions, so it is important we fill our minds with uplifting and charitable *thoughts*. This is especially true of leadership past and present.

We are strengthened by thinking on Christ and are helped by such thoughts to overcome temptations. Also, by letting virtue garnish our thoughts we increase our understanding of the doctrines of the Priesthood which is the governing and saving power of Christ.

Our thoughts are power unto salvation. As has been said, "sew a *thought*," and after all is said and done—"reap an eternal destiny."

❧

CAN WE BE PERFECTED ALONE?

———

One Sunday a Bishop was giving a special lesson to the Relief Society called, "Recognizing Blessings." During the course of the lesson the Bishop repeatedly taught that they should never do anything in or out of the Church without first asking, "What's in it for me?, meaning what blessings are in it for me?

Though his intentions were good, the principles were wrong. A self-centered attitude will never get us closer to the Lord and his selfless life.

What did the Savior teach both in principle and by example?

Thought Seventy-six
AS WE ARE ONE

In 1 Corinthians 13:5 we are taught that,

> "...(Charity) seeketh not her own..."

Again we are taught in John 17:21-23:

> "That they all may be one; as thou, Father, art in me, and I in thee, that they also may be one in us: ...And the glory which thou gavest me I have given them; that they may be one, even as we are one: I in them, and thou in me, that they may be made perfect in one:..."

In the pre-existence we were all part of the glory of our Heavenly Father.[1] Then there arose a division among the *intelligences or kingdom of God*, and we lost one-third of the host of heaven.

Here on earth, we are not only separated from our Savior, but again we are experiencing a division among His children. Our challenge is to again become one, spiritually, through Christ and return to our Heavenly Father.

1. D&C 93:36, Abraham 3:22, also *100 Easy Thought Talks for LDS Youth,* Vol. I, pp.18.

———◆———

Thought Seventy-seven
ESTEEM OUR BROTHER

Though we are physically separated from the Lord on this earth, He is not far away. Acts 17:27 & 28 explains:

> "That they should seek the Lord, if haply they might feel after him, and find him, *though he be not far from every one of us: For in him we live, and move, and have our being;* as certain also of your poets have said, For we are also his offspring."

See also D&C 88:6-13.

Because of the possible danger we face of being permanently separated from Him and one another, the Lord teaches us to *esteem our brother as ourselves.* D&C 38:24-25 & 27 say:

> "And let every man esteem his brother as himself, and practice virtue and holiness before me. And again I say unto you, let every man esteem his brother as himself...I say unto you, be one; and if ye are not one ye are not mine."

In esteeming others as ourselves, we become spiritually one, and by so doing, become Christ's.

Thought Seventy-eight
THE IMPORTANCE OF ZION

We are taught to seek to establish Zion. D&C 14:6 records:

> "Seek to bring forth and establish my Zion. Keep my commandments in all things."

In Moses 7:18 we are told why. It says:

> "And the Lord called his people Zion, because they were of one heart and one mind, and dwelt in righteousness; and there were no poor among them."

If we seek to establish Zion, then we are seeking to become of one heart and one mind, and many blessings attend us as we do. 1 Nephi 13:37 explains:

> "And blessed are they who shall seek to bring forth my Zion at that day, for they shall have the gift and the power of the Holy Ghost; and if they endure unto the end they shall be lifted up at the last day, and shall be saved in the everlasting kingdom of the Lamb; and whoso shall publish peace, yea, tidings of great joy, how beautiful upon the mountains shall they be."

This important *principle* of becoming one is so essential for our success here on earth that all through the scriptures we are refocused on Zion.

Jesus, even in teaching us how to pray, shows us the importance of Zion. Matthew 6:9 & 10 records:

> "After this manner therefore pray ye: Our Father which art in heaven, Hallowed be thy name. *Thy kingdom come. Thy will be done in earth, as it is in heaven.*"

After He addresses the Father, to identify who we are in relation to God, and glorifies Him by saying, "Hallowed be thy name," the first blessing he prayed for was Zion to be established.

"Thy kingdom come, thy will be done in earth, as it is in heaven." He was praying for Zion. We are to also pray for the establishment of Zion as well as strive for it by loving one another.

Thought Seventy-nine

SATAN KNOWS THE IMPORTANCE OF ZION

Satan knows we are to become *spiritually one* to become like Heavenly Father. He also knows he cannot conquer us while we are unified.

Just as an arrow, by itself, can be easily broken, so can we. But a thick bundle of arrows together, or many of us united, cannot be so easily broken. Therefore, it is Satan's desire to separate us from each other and Heavenly Father.

He knows he can isolate us through *philosophies* of men which teach us to change *we* to *me*. This gives him an advantage over us.

In 2 Corinthians 2, Paul counters this philosophy by teaching the Saints to love and forgive one another in order to prevent the contentions that would divide them. Verses 5-11 say:

> "But if any have caused grief...Sufficient to such a man is this punishment, which was inflicted of many. So that contrariwise ye ought rather to forgive him, and comfort

him, lest perhaps such a one should be swallowed up with overmuch sorrow. Wherefore I beseech you that ye would confirm your love toward him…Lest Satan should get an advantage of us: for we are not ignorant of his devices."

We aren't ignorant of the devices being used zealously today that would cause division among us.

Thought Eighty
WHAT'S IN IT FOR ME?

One of the devices of Satan is a philosophy which advocates—"First ask, What's in it for me?" This teaches us to center on selfish attainments, intimating that a self-centered focus increases our chances for success. But we are warned not to seek things for ourselves in Jeremiah 45:5 which says:

> "And seekest thou great things for thyself? seek them not: for, behold, I will bring evil upon all flesh, saith the Lord: but thy life will I give unto thee for a prey in all places whither thou goest."

The philosophies Satan uses such as *"look out for #1, avoid emotional bankruptcy,* or *avoid coming out on the short-end,"* claim they are trying to help us *gain control of our lives and prosper our cause.*

However, they only serve to make us enemies of ourselves, each other, and most of all, God. Remember that Satan is the Father of lies and deception. Romans 10:2-3 says:

> "For I bear them record that they have a zeal of God, but not according to knowledge. For they being ignorant of God's righteousness, and going about to establish their own righteousness, have not submitted themselves unto the righteousness of God."

Satan is trying to establish his own definition of righteousness which divides us. Whereas God is establishing His *righteousness* to unite us into oneness or perfection.

Thought Eighty-one
GOD'S RIGHTEOUSNESS

Remember, *Godly knowledge* really connotes intelligence, otherwise it "vanishes away."[1] for it is of this earth.

Knowledge of this earth focuses on self. Therefore, knowledge, ignorant of God's *righteousness*, is self-centered. Self-centeredness fights against Zion. 2 Nephi 10:16 says:

> "Wherefore, he that fighteth against Zion, both Jew and Gentile, both bond and free, both male and female, shall perish; for they are they who are the whore of all the earth; for they who are not for me are against me,saith our God."

If we receive truth we will not be found ignorant of God's *righteousness* or fighting against Zion. The people of Nephi, the son of Helaman, refused it. Helaman 10:17 & 18 say:

> "And it came to pass that thus he (Nephi) did go forth in the Spirit, from multitude to multitude, declaring the word of God, even until he had declared it unto them all, or sent it forth among all the people. And it came to pass that they would not hearken unto his words and there began to be contentions insomuch that they were divided against themselves and began to slay one another with the sword."

When truth is rejected, the people become divided against one another.

1. 1 Corinthians 13:8, also *100 Easy Thought Talks for LDS Youth,* Vol. I, pp.37-38.

RECEIVE TRUTH THROUGH THE HOLY GHOST

D&C 45:57 says:

> "For they that are wise and have received the truth, and have taken the Holy Spirit for their guide, and have not been deceived—verily I say unto you, they shall not be hewn down and cast into the fire, but shall abide the day."

If we are wise, we receive truth by witness of the Holy Ghost, otherwise we may be deceived, taking the philosophies of men for truth. Moroni 10:5 says:

> "And by the power of the Holy Ghost ye may know the truth of all things."

Thought Eighty-three
LOVE AND PEACE

We can search the scriptures and learn of our true purpose on this earth. This gives us control of our lives and prospers our cause in *God's righteousness*.

In God's righteousness we repent and are cleansed from sin and given a new heart. In this we gain *charity* in service, understanding, and forgiveness one for another. In these we add to our *glory*, which is *oneness* in Christ.

There isn't anything *in it for us* in the worldly sense, but we are promised something much greater, *"the God of love and peace shall be with us."* 2 Corinthians 13:11 says:

> "Finally, brethren, farewell. Be perfect, be of good comfort, be of one mind, live in peace; and the God of love and peace shall be with you."

Remember that Christ is our *righteousness or perfection* through our humble, repentant submission to Him, so Paul teaches us to be perfect through Christ. He knows that this makes us one with God, and that in this unity we will find comfort, love, and peace.

———◆———

Thought Eighty-four
WE AFFECT OTHERS

Some mistakenly believe that what they do will not affect anyone but themselves.

We hear them say, "It's my life, not yours." But the scriptures teach us that we are all inseparately connected as children of our Heavenly Father. Acts 17:28 records:

> "For in him we live, and move, and have our being; as certain also of your poets have said, for *we are also His offspring.*"

Just like any family, we cannot be added upon or taken away from without making us either stronger or weaker.

So, those who think they can do *anything because it's their life*, bring selfishness to both earthly and heavenly families. They infect them with spiritual disease by the philosophies which claim to be the cures. D&C 2:2 & 3 warns us:

> "And he shall plant in the hearts of the children the promises made to the fathers, and the hearts of the children shall turn to their fathers. If it were not so, the whole earth would be utterly wasted at his coming."

Our actions are not without affect. William James said it this way:

> Act as if what you do makes a difference. It does.

———◆———

Thought Eighty-five
SELF-DENIAL IS THE TRUE CURE

If centering ourselves in Christ strengthens our *love, or intelligence,* then it follows that we cannot be at the center, serving self, without decreasing our light of *intelligence.*

Also, by fighting against the Lord's purpose of bringing about Zion or oneness, we give Satan power over us. Self-denial is the only power which can save us. Mark 8:34-36 says:

> "And when he had called the people unto him with his disciples also he said unto them, Whosoever will come after me, *let him deny himself,* and take up his cross, and follow me. *For whosoever will save his life shall lose it; but whosoever shall lose his life for my sake and the gospel's the same shall save it.* For what shall it profit a man, if he shall gain the whole world, and lose his own soul? Or what shall a man give in exchange for his soul?"

Only in doing the opposite of what the world advocates can we overcome the world and be one with Heavenly Father.

———

Thought Eighty-six
THE NATURAL MAN IS AN ENEMY TO GOD

In knowing God's purpose to unite us, we understand why the natural man, being selfish and carnal, is an enemy to God. We also can see the need to be reborn. Mosiah 3:19 says:

> "For the natural man is an enemy to God, and has been from the fall of Adam, and will be, forever and ever, *unless he yields to the enticings of the Holy Spirit, and putteth off the natural man and becometh a saint through the atonement of Christ the Lord,* and becometh as a child, submissive, meek, humble, patient, full of love, willing to submit to all things which the Lord seeth fit to inflict upon him, even as a child doth submit to his father."

We also understand why, if we do everything with ourselves as the main focus, we ultimately lose the battle against this enemy to God. Brigham Young said it this way.

> "Instead of seeking unto the Lord for wisdom, they seek unto vain philosophy and the deceit and traditions of men, which are after the rudiments of the world and not after Christ. They are led by their own imaginations and by the dictates of their selfish will, which will lead them in the end to miss the object of their pursuit. (*Brigham Young Discourses* 10:209)"

Thought Eighty-seven
TRUSTING IN OURSELVES

We are nothing or powerless in and of ourselves. Since we can do nothing without the strength of God, we will only allow this world to overcome us by centering on ourselves and eliminating God from our main focus. 2 Nephi 4:34 says;

> "O Lord, I have trusted in thee and I will trust in thee forever, I will not put my trust in the arm of flesh; for I know that cursed is he that putteth his trust in the arm of flesh. Yea, cursed is he that putteth his trust in man or maketh flesh his arm."

We often have the perspective that we must do it all for ourselves or it won't get done. In other words, we *"trust in our own arm of flesh."*

This is a philosophy of Satan. It not only isolates us from each other but isolates us from the one we profess to worship; God. Matthew 6:33 says:

> "Seek ye *first* the kingdom of God, and his righteousness; and all these things shall be added unto you."

Our faith in the Lord and the power it brings to our lives can be destroyed by self-centeredness. Matthew 6:30-33 say:

> "Wherefore, if God so clothed the grass of the field, shall he not much more clothe you...O ye of little faith?

Therefore take no thought, saying what shall we eat? or What shall we drink? or, Wherewithal shall we be clothed? (For after all these things do the Gentiles seek:) for your heavenly Father knoweth that ye have need of all these things. But *seek ye first the kingdom of God, and His righteousness;* and all these things shall be added unto you."

If we center on God, He can bring about *our righteousness,* showing us His powerful love in every aspect of our lives.

———◆———

PART IS INCOMPLETE OR IMPERFECT

Remember, the glory or intelligence that we are constitutes the kingdom of God in us. We are part of God's kingdom.[1]

"Part" means that we, all by ourselves, are incomplete or imperfect. Zion, or the Kingdom of God coming is based on our uniting all parts into one complete whole or being made perfect. 1 Corinthians 12:14,20,25-27 say:

> "For as the body is one, and hath many members, and all the members of that one body, being many, are one body: so also is Christ. For by one Spirit are we all baptized into one body, whether we be Jews or Gentiles, whether we be bond or free; and have been all made to drink into one Spirit. For the body is not one member, but many... That there should be no schism in the body; but that the members should have the same care one for another. And whether one member suffer, all the members suffer with it; or one member be honoured, all the members rejoice with it. Now ye are the body of Christ, and members in particular."

Therefore we are not our own, but a working part of Christ. So, when we are adding to our intelligence or glory, we are putting the kingdom of God first. This is done by seeking the Father's will, not our own.

Christ always sought to do the will of His Father. John 6:38 records:

"For I came down from heaven, not to do mine own will, but the will of him that sent me."

It is by doing the will of the Father that we seek the kingdom of God. He wants us to be elevated to a unified frame of mind, increasing in love as we continue seeking the good of all.

1. Luke 17:20-21, also *100 Easy Thought Talks for LDS Youth*, Vol. I, pp. 50

Thought Eighty-nine
FAMILIES ARE FOREVER

We are all inseparably connected through our Father in Heaven, thereby giving us reason to call each other brothers and sisters, the same as earthly families.

Even the work that we do for the dead makes our pre-existent and earthly connections continue forever. *This is keeping an eternal perspective, or an eye single.* Luke 11:34 says:

"The light of the body is the eye: therefore when thine eye is single the whole body also is full of light: but when thine eye is evil, thy body also is full of darkness."

This refers to our spiritual eyes. If our eyes are single, we will be one in heart, mind and purpose, thus filling us with light which is intelligence or glory,[1] even as the Father and Son are one and full of glory. John 17:21-23 say:

"That they all may be one; as thou, Father, art in me, and I in thee, that they also may be one in us: ...And the glory which thou gavest me I have given them; that they may be one, even as we are one: I in them, and thou in me, that they may be made perfect in one:..."

So keeping our eye single, or unified, makes our families, both heavenly and earthly, one and forever through Christ.

1 D&C 93:36-37; also *100 Easy Talk Thoughts for LDS Youth*, Vol. I, p.18

Thought Ninety
WHAT'S THE DIFFERENCE?

Since we have the kingdom of God, or glory in us, some might think looking out for #1 and *seeking the kingdom of God first,* means the same thing, but they do not.

Looking out for #1 is of Satan, advocating self-centeredness is totally opposite to uniting our glory with other's, which is what Christ advocates. Alma 5:40-41 says:

> "For I say unto you that whatsoever is good cometh from God, and whatsoever is evil cometh from the devil. Therefore, if a man bringeth forth good works he hearkeneth unto the voice of the good shepherd and he doth follow him; but whatsoever bringeth forth evil works, the same becometh a child of the devil, for he hearkeneth unto his voice, and doth follow him."

By seeking the kingdom of God, we seek the good of everyone as a whole, and give ourselves up to spiritual oneness. If we seek selfish pursuits we serve the wrong master.

Thought Ninety-one
LOVE ONE ANOTHER

The Lord's way to solve any problem we have, is for us to focus on Him and His will. Asking "What would Jesus do?" instead of "What's in it for me?" In this way we are following Him. John 15:12 says:

> "This is my commandment, That ye love one another, as I have loved you."

The way He loved us was with *charity* or His pure love. Therefore, we are to love one another the same way. In John

21:15 we are shown just how important Christ felt that love was. It records:

> "So when they had dined, Jesus saith to Simon Peter, Simon, son of Jonas, lovest thou me more than these? He saith unto him, Yea, Lord; thou knowest that I love thee. He saith into him, Feed my lambs."

Jesus goes on to ask Peter twice more if he loves Him, and then afterward charges him to feed his sheep. By so doing, he was trying to impress upon Peter the vital need of love or charity in serving one another.

Thought Ninety-two
FOR THE NEXT LIFE

This life is not made for this life, but for the life to come. It is an opportunity to grow in glory and intelligence, that could not be procured in any other way.

Admittedly, it is sometimes confusing and difficult, but its the challenge which works for our spiritual growth.

Unfortunately, the world takes advantage of our confusion and tries to teach Satan's ways to make us lose our eternal perspective.

However, to follow Satan's way is like putting our money into a piece of pottery and burying it in the earth, instead of into a bank that is known to last *and give interest*. Matthew 6:19-21 say:

> "Lay not up for yourselves treasures upon earth where moth and rust doth corrupt, and where thieves break through and steal: But lay up for yourselves treasures in heaven, where neither moth nor rust doth corrupt, and where thieves do not break through nor steal: For where your treasure is, there will your heart be also."

The life after this is eternal. It not only will last forever, but it can pay incredible dividends, if we are *righteous. Guaranteed.*

Thought Ninety-three
THE UNSEEN

Again, we must examine our hearts[1] and see what we have treasured up in them. If they are self-serving, we are investing in perishable goods with no guarantees.

Sometimes we find this difficult here, since those things promised eternally are unseen. Matthew 13:44 says:

> "Again, the kingdom of heaven is like unto treasure *hid* in a field; the which when a man hath found, he hideth, and for joy thereof goeth and selleth all that he hath and buyeth that field."

Though the treasure isn't readily visible, once found, it is the most valuable of all treasures, enough so as to influence a man into selling all he has to obtain it.

This treasure is only found by keeping our focus on God who is unseen, not ourselves who are seen. 2 Corinthians 4:18 says:

> "While we look not at the things which are seen, but at the things which are not seen: for the things which are seen are temporal; but the things which are not seen are eternal."

1. 2 Corinthians 13:5, also *100 Easy Thought Talks for LDS Youth*, Vol. I, pp.39-40

Thought Ninety-four
WARN OUR NEIGHBOR

It is part of the plan that the treasure be difficult to find so that when we have found it, we will have to help others to find it also. D&C 88:81 & 83 say:

> "Behold, I sent you out to testify and warn the people, and it becometh every man who hath been warned to warn his

neighbor.... He that seeketh me early shall find me, and shall not be forsaken."

We cannot only seek our own salvation because it is in bringing others with us that we receive it. In fact, we are to wear out our lives exposing the deceitful philosophies that keep the treasure from being found. D&C 123:13 says:

> "Therefore that we should waste and wear out our lives in bringing to light all the hidden things of darkness, where in we know them; and they are truly manifest from heaven--"

We must become aware and warn others to not be swayed by philosophies which would divide our Father's kingdom with selfishness. Mark 3:24 says:

> "And if a kingdom be divided against itself, that kingdom cannot stand."

In other words, spiritual unity or being one is not just an eternal pre-requisite, it is essential for us to stand and progress.

We cannot seek our own and progress in a kingdom which is the very epitome of unity and oneness.

WHY MUST WE DEPEND ON THE LORD?

A young Elders's Quorum president was struggling to fill all the needs of the people under his stewardship. But the load was so great that many of the other elders and their wives were starting to complain and develop negative feelings one for another. The valiant efforts of this diligent leader were commendable, but a total failure.

When he sat with his wise bishop in counsel, he was asked just one question, "Did you submit the needs of your quorum to the Lord, and then execute your efforts from and through His will and strength? He had to answer no.

Thought Ninety-five
TRUST NOT IN THE ARM OF FLESH

We are exhorted to not put our trust in the arm of flesh, but rather trust in the Lord. 2 Nephi 4:34 says:

> "O Lord, I have trusted in thee, and I will trust in thee forever. I will not put my trust in the arm of flesh; for I know that cursed is he that putteth his trust in the arm of flesh. Yea, cursed is he that putteth his trust in man or maketh flesh his arm."

This means we are not to depend on men or their wisdom, but depend upon the power of God. 1 Corinthians 2:5 says:

> "That your faith should not stand in the wisdom of men, but in the power of God."

Thought Ninety-six
AS SERVANTS OF THE LORD

Men have not created us, nor given us this earth. So, why would we have faith in men? Mosiah taught in Mosiah 2:21 that we are dependent on the Lord for everything. It says:

> "I say unto you that if ye should serve him who has created you from the beginning, and is preserving you from day to day, by lending you breath, that ye may live and move and do according to your own will, and even supporting you from one moment to another—I say, if ye should serve him with all your whole souls yet ye would be unprofitable servants."

In everything we do, if we remember where our strength comes from, and draw upon it diligently, we will not be frustrated in our efforts to serve the Lord and our fellowmen. 2 Nephi 32:9 says:

> "But behold, I say unto you that ye must pray always, and not faint; that ye must not perform any thing unto the

Lord save in the first place ye shall pray unto the Father in the name of Christ, that he will consecrate thy performance unto thee, that thy performance may be for the welfare of thy soul."

Other references: Proverbs 16:3, Jeremiah 44:8, 48:7 and Psalms 127:1.

Thought Ninety-seven
WE LEARN FROM MOSES' EXPERIENCE

It has been thought that if we are obeying the Lords will, that we are automatically going to be blessed in accomplishing it. Not so. We must also include the Lord by relying on his strength to accomplish it.

Moses felt he was to help free his brethren, and learned that on his own, without the Lord's help, he couldn't accomplish even his worthy goals. Exodus 2:11-12 & 15 records Moses' experience as he observed the abusive treatment of his people. Exodus 2:11-12 & 15 records:

> "And it came to pass in those days, when Moses was grown, that he went out unto his brethren, and looked on their burdens: and he spied an Egyptian smiting an Hebrew, one of his brethren. And he looked this way and that way, and when he saw that there was no man, he slew the Egyptian, and hid him in the sand...Now when Pharaoh heard this thing, he sought to slay Moses, But Moses Fled from the face of Pharaoh, and dwelt in the land of Midian..."

Even though his desire was honorable and it was the will of the Lord that he help free his people, without the help of the Lord, he only made things worse.

It took many years for Moses to come to the Lord and receive of His power. But after he did, he was able to free all his people. Exodus 12:41 which says:

"And it came to pass at the end of the four hundred and thirty years, even the selfsame day it came to pass, that all the hosts of the Lord went out from the land of Egypt."

Not only were all the Israelites freed, but they were allowed to take the spoils of Egypt with them. Exodus 12:32 & 35-37 records:

"Also take your flocks and your herds, as ye have said, and he gone; and bless me also...And the children of Israel did according to the word of Moses; and they borrowed (ask for) of the Egyptians jewels of silver, and jewels of gold, and raiment: And the Lord gave the people favor in the sight of the Egyptians, so that they lent unto them such things as they required. And they spoiled the Egyptians."

———◆———

Thought Ninety-eight
NEPHI

Nephi also learned the difference it made to work with the power of God. Nephi was commanded to return to Jerusalem, along with his brothers, to obtain the brass plates. 1 Nephi 3:4 records:

"Wherefore, the Lord hath commanded me that thou and thy brothers should go unto the house of Laban, and seek the records, and bring them down hither into the wilderness."

They even decided to purchase the records, but again without the Lord's guidance. 1 Nephi 3:22-25 records:

"And we cast lots—who of us should go in unto the house of Laban. And it came to pass that the lot fell upon Laman; and Laman went in unto the house of Laban, and he talked with him as he sat in his house. And he desired of Laban the records which were engraven upon the plates of brass, which contained the genealogy of my father. And behold, it came to pass that Laban was angry, and thrust him out from his presence; and he would not that he should have the records. Wherefore, he said unto him: Behold thou art a robber, and I will slay thee."

Even though it was the Lord's will they obtain the plates, their own efforts to get the plates, without the Lord's help, failed. First Laman tried. 1 Nephi 3:11-12 says:

> "And it came to pass that we went down to the land of our inheritance, and we did gather together our gold, and our silver, and our precious things. And after we had gathered these things together, we went up again unto the house of Laban. And it came to pass that we went in unto Laban, and desired him that he would give unto us the records which were engraven upon the plates of brass, for which we would give unto him our gold, and our silver, and all our precious things. And it came to pass that when Laban saw our property, and that it was exceedingly great, he did lust after it, insomuch that he thrust us out, and sent his servants to slay us, that he might obtain our property."

Not only did they fail again to gain possession of the plates, but they lost all of their property to Laban. 1 Nephi 3:26 says:

> "And it came to pass that we did flee before the servants of Laban, and we were obliged to leave behind our property, and it fell into the hands of Laban."

After this and a visit from an angel Nephi allowed himself to be led by the Spirit. 1 Nephi 4:6-7 in part says:

> "And I was led by the Spirit, not knowing before hand the things which I should do. Nevertheless I went forth…"

With the Lord guiding him, he was able to *safely and successfully* obtain the plates and the servant of Laban and return to the tent of his father. 1 Nephi 4:38 says:

> "And it came to pass that we took the plates of brass and the servant of Laban, and departed into the wilderness, and journeyed unto the tent of our father."

———

Thought Ninety-nine
THE LORD WORKS IN MYSTERIOUS WAYS

There is a hymn we sing on page 285 of the hymnal which declares:

> "God Works in a mysterious way His wonders to perform."

An example of this is found in 2 Chronicles 20:1-30. Here King Jehoshaphat was warned of three nations coming to battle against him. 2 Chronicles 20:1-2 says:

> "It came to pass after this also, that the children of Moab, and the children of Ammon, and with them other beside the Ammonites, came against Jehoshaphat to battle. Then there came some that told Jehoshaphat, saying, There cometh a great multitude against thee from beyond the sea on this side Syria...."

Because Jehoshaphat was wise enough to recognize his limitations as a man, he immediately sought for the Lord's help by having his people fast. 2 Chronicles 20:3 records:

> "And Jehoshaphat feared, and set himself to seek the Lord, and proclaimed a fast throughout all Judah."

When they came together as a people they prayed. In answer to their prayers, a Levite standing among them received a wonderful revelation from the Lord. 2 Chronicles 20:15-17 records:

> "And he said, Hearken ye, all Judah, and ye inhabitance of Jerusalem, and thou king Jehoshaphat, Thus saith the Lord unto you, Be not afraid nor dismayed by reason of this great multitude: for the battle is not yours, but God's...Ye shall not need to fight in this battle; set yourselves, stand ye still, and see the salvation of the Lord with you, O Judah and Jerusalem: fear not, nor be dismayed; tomorrow go out against them; for the Lord will be with you."

When the battle was to take place, the three enemy armies came upon each other in the wilderness. And all the people of Judah had to do was stand on a hill nearby singing praises to God. At this point, they watched as the Lord fought their battle by having their enemies slay each other. 2 Chronicles 20:22-23 records:

> "And when they began to sing and to praise, the Lord set ambushments against the children of Ammon, Moab, and mount Seir, which were come against Judah; and they were smitten; for the children of Ammon and Moab stood up against the inhabitants of mount Seir, utterly to slay and destroy them: and when they had made an end of the inhabitants of Seir, every one helped to destroy another."

Again, as with the children of Israel, the people of Judah not only were rescued from their enemies in a miraculous way, but they were able to take all the spoils of a battle in which they didn't have to fight. 2 Chronicles 20:24-25 says:

> "And when Judah came toward the watch tower in the wilderness, they looked unto the multitude, and, behold, they were dead bodies fallen to the earth, and none escaped. And when Jehosphat and his people came to take away the spoil of them, they found among them in abundance both riches with the dead bodies, and precious jewels, which they striped off for themselves, more than they could carry away: and they were three days in gathering of the spoil, it was so much."

Thought One Hundred
PROCLAMATIONS OF FAITH

In order for these great leaders to have the help of the Lord, they had to not only declair their faith through submission to His will, but they also had to actively demonstrate it through total submission to the Lord, Himself.

Nephi proclaimed he knew that the Lord would make whatever He commanded possible, and thus he would willingly submit to the Lord's will. 1 Nephi 3:7 says:

"And it came to pass that I, Nephi, said unto my father: I will go and do the things which the Lord hath commanded, for I know that the Lord giveth no commandments unto the children of men, save he shall prepare a way for them that they may accomplish the thing which he commandeth them."

Also, Nephi was given a promise of success from his father. 1 Nephi 3:6 records;

"Therefore go, my son, and thou shalt be favored of the Lord, because thou hast not murmured."

However, it wasn't until he totally left himself physically vulnerable and put his trust in the hands of the Lord that he had success. 1 Nephi 4:6-7 in part says:

"And I was led by the Spirit, not knowing before hand the things which I should do. Nevertheless I went forth..."

Jehoshphat also proclaimed his confidence in the Lord, not only in the fasting, but in the prayer he uttered before the people of Judah. 2 Chronicles 20:7-9 records this prayer:

"Art not thou our God, who didst drive out the inhabitants of this land before thy people Israel, and gavest it to the seed of Abraham thy friend forever? And they dwelt therein, and have built thee a sanctuary therein for thy name, saying, If, when evil cometh upon us, as the sword, judgment, or pestilence, or famine, we stand before this house, and in thy presence, (for thy name is in this house,) and cry unto thee in our affliction, then thou wilt hear and help."

However, it wasn't until they stood upon the mount and sang praises to the Lord, putting themselves in a seemingly vulnerable position, that they placed themselves in the hands of the Lord, which *allowed His power to help* them succeed.